TIMELESS

22 LESSONS OF FAITH, HOPE & LOVE

TIMELESS

22 LESSONS OF FAITH, HOPE & LOVE

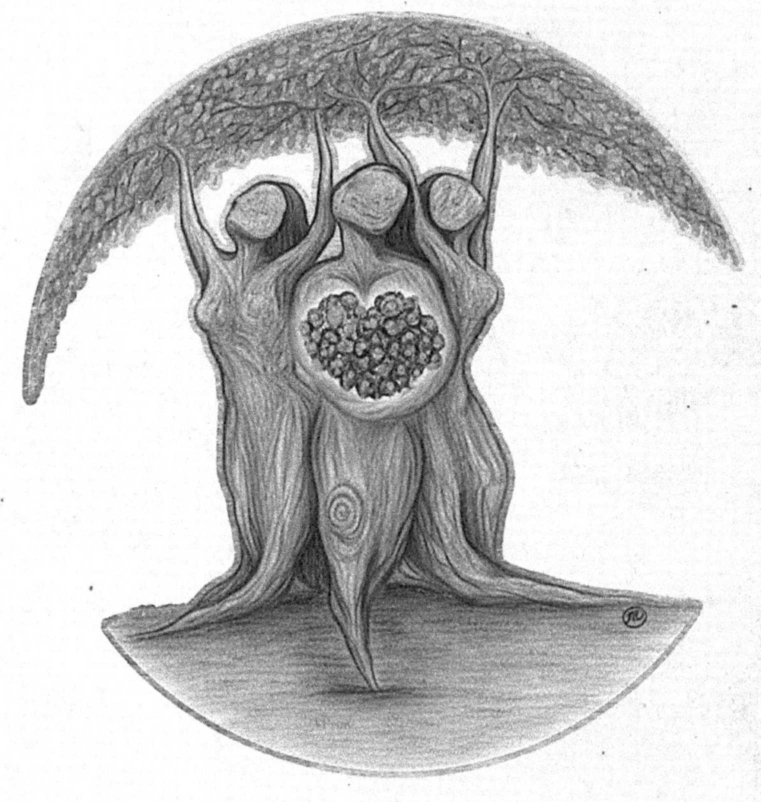

DEADRA WOODS STOKES

TIMELESS: 22 Lessons of Faith, Hope, & Love

ISBN: 979-8-9941726-0-5

LCCN: 2026900124

Published by: Stokes Legacy Group, LLC.

Cover Illustration: Patricia Nash of P'Nash Peach Artflow
Cover Design: The 20/20 Brand
Internal Layout and Design: InSCRIBEd Inspiration, LLC.

Printed in the United States of America

All real-life anecdotes are told with permission from actual parties involved and recorded to the best of the author's recollection. Names in some instances have not been used at the request of the individuals referenced. In some cases, parties mentioned are deceased. Details of some instances have been slightly modified to enhance readability, or to ensure privacy. Any resemblance of any other parties is purely coincidental.

DEDICATION

This book is dedicated to the women who came before me and the generations who will follow; it is written in gratitude, remembrance and love.

Mom, **Barbara J. Woods**, your faith, discipline, intellect, and unwavering commitment to service shaped the woman I have become. Your lessons were lived, not lectured, and your example continues to guide me daily.

My grandmothers, **Mary Nealy Little** and **Juanita Love Sanders**, whose resilience, sacrifice, and quiet strength laid the foundation for our family. You taught me the value of hard work, land, legacy, and love long before I understood their power.

FOREWORD: A COVERING FOR TIMELESS

*Those who respect their elders pave
their own road towards success.*

\- African Proverb

In 2025 a small group of students from Trinity United Church of Christ traveled to Senegal and The Gambia and had the blessed opportunity to stand in the Door of No Return on Goree Island. Each student wrote a letter to an ancestor they never met, to say Thank You for their resilience, faithfulness, ambition, and determination. As the students debriefed about the experience, some holding back tears, they collectively communicated a single idea - how grateful they all were for the sacrifices of the elders in their family, as one student stated, "for the first time I feel connected to Africa and my roots in Alabama."

The goal of the trip was to expand the vision of these young people and help them to understand the extraordinary struggles and brilliant creativity embedded in their culture. *Timeless* eeks the same outcome for you to recognize the timeless wisdom found in beautiful stories, engraved upon the souls of the women who shaped the life of one Deadra Stokes.

In this memoir, devotional, and prayer journal, you will discover the story of a tenacious, unyielding, and loving woman named Mary Nealy Little. Grandma Mary, as she was called, dared to accomplish the impossible in a state where domestic terror was legal called Mississippi. Grandma Mary dared to become a landowner. Not an ordinary landowner, but the magistrate of 80 prime acres of rich, black soil. This was an act of faith and tenacity.

In these pages you will discover the story of a quiet revolutionary named, Juanita Love Saunders whose very spirit empowered economically and spiritually, the lineage of Deadra Stokes' family. You will fall in love with the gracious spirit of Barbara Jean Woods, whose motherly smile could make the devil think twice about doing wrong. Deadra has crafted a womanist homage honoring the people whose shoulders she stands upon. May these *Timeless Lessons* of faith, hope, and love bless your life, and may you pass on the wisdom of these amazing women to those you love.

Rev. Dr. Otis Moss, III

Trinity United Church of Christ, Pastor

ACKNOWLEDGEMENTS

This book was written through community, sustained by prayer, and carried forward by love. While the lessons in these pages are rooted in the lives of my Mothers, this work was made possible by many people who walked alongside me, encouraged me, and held me up throughout this journey.

I begin with my husband, **Paul**, your steady presence and unwavering support are a constant source of strength. No matter the task I attempt to conquer, he stands with me, prays with me, and prays over me. He is a devoted partner and the greatest girl dad I could have ever chosen for our daughters.

My daughters, **Sydney, Malaika and Nya,** you make me proud every day. Thank you for believing in me and supporting my dreams. Your love, encouragement, and grace inspire me more than you know.

The vision, courage, compassion, and leadership of my current pastor, **Reverend Otis Moss, III**, continues to feed my spirit and inspires me to grow spiritually.

My Executive Pastor, sorority sister, and prayer warrior, **Reverend Stacey Dunn**. You were a faithful presence and one of my mother's special surrogate daughters who showered her with love. Your care and devotion will always be remembered.

My mother-in-law, **Bobbie Jean Stokes**. You set an example through hard work, perseverance, and entrepreneurship. Watching you roll up her sleeves and build a bakery business that served the community for more than thirty years made a lasting impression on me.

My best friend, advisor, sorority sister, and unwavering supporter, **Jeanne Charles**. You offered steadfast dedication, encouragement, and motivation. Your guidance, belief in me, and willingness to walk with me in every season has meant more than words can express.

After more than thirty-nine plus years of shared life, sisterhood, and friendship, I am grateful for my **15 line sisters**. We continue to cheer one another on, offer daily prayers, and speak encouragement from the sidelines. Our bond is a blessing I do not take lightly.

Aunt Susie, **Aunt Ilet**, and **Aunt Malree**, thank you for trusting me with your personal memories of Grandma Mary. Your willingness to share those intimate moments enriched this work and honored her legacy.

Cousin Clara, you shared special memories working with Grandma Mary on the farm. Your reflections brought her story to life in a meaningful way.

My sister-in-law, **Jimia Stokes,** thank you for the tenderness and love you showed my momma during her final moments. Your kindness during that sacred time will forever remain in my heart.

LaTanya Law, thank you for checking on me and walking me through grief. Your understanding and compassion have been a steady source of comfort.

To my sister, **Penda L. Jame**s, and InSCRIBEd Inspiration, thank you for coaching me with wisdom and purpose and helping me cross the finish line.

My line sister, **Shellie,** and her dear mother, **Geneva**, thank you for your thoughtful review and assistance with final edits. You helped bring this work to completion.

Patricia Nash, thank you for taking the time to truly hear my story and allowing it to inspire such a beautiful cover design.

Above all, I give thanks to **God Almighty**. Every lesson, every word, and every step of this journey is grounded in His grace, sustained by His mercy, and guided by His love. To Him be all the glory.

TIMELESS

22 LESSONS OF FAITH, HOPE & LOVE

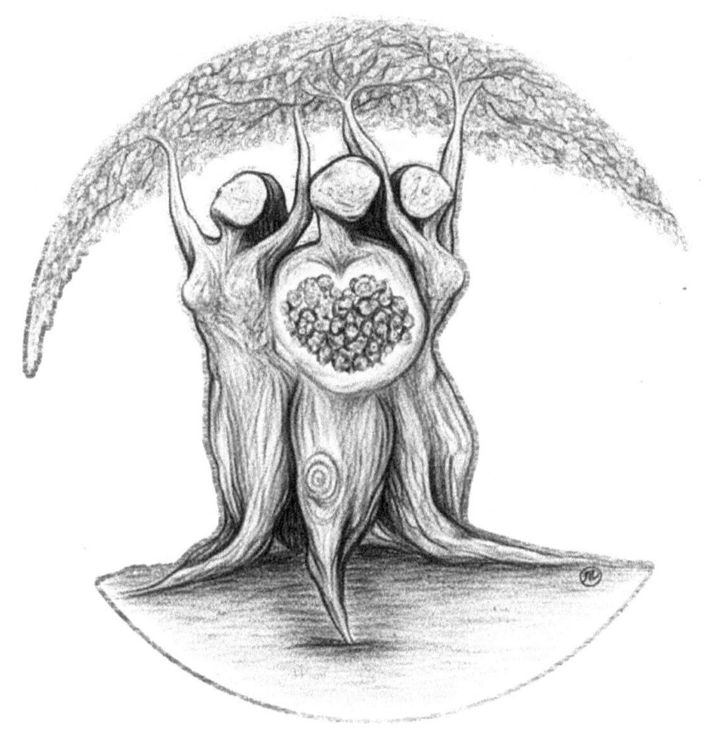

"The women who raised me built cathedrals without bricks —with faith, discipline, and love."

- Deadra W. Stokes

INTRODUCTION
Lessons Lived, Lessons Carried

Some lessons come from classrooms. Others are whispered over kitchen tables, offered through quiet gestures, or spoken in love at the right moment. The deepest lessons I ever learned weren't written in textbooks, they were lived out by the women who raised me. I was enrolled in a living curriculum rooted in faith, resilience, and intentional legacy. From Mississippi's red clay to Chicago's crowded streets; from cleaning other people's homes to directing community programs, my Mothers "Grandma Mary," Mary Nealy Little; "Granny" Juanita Love Sanders; and "Mom" Barbara Jean Woods modeled what it means to build something that lasts.

No matter what titles they held beyond their front doors, their most sacred title was always "Mother." Whether they were mentoring co-workers, welcoming grandchildren, or feeding neighbors, their message never changed: family first. They believed success means little if the next generation isn't stronger because of it. They loved with boundaries, disciplined with purpose, and sacrificed without complaint so that generations after them could walk through doors they once only imagined.

Standing On Their Shoulders

As I stand on the threshold of my sixth decade, I see their fingerprints everywhere, in my resilience, determination, discipline, and most of all, faith. They didn't just survive; they built, planned, and prepared. Their legacy lives not only in the land we still walk upon, or the homes we still own, but in every decision that places faith over fear, family over ego, and future over convenience.

I am not merely the recipient of their legacy, I am its steward. And through me, their lessons continue to move, evolve, and bless others. I came to realize that legacy is not what you leave behind, legacy is what you build every day of your life. We are the prayers of our mothers, our aunties, our sisters, or the special women walking, building, and believing around us.

Carrying Their Legacy Forward

The legacy of my Mothers did not end with their lives. It lives on in how I lead, how I serve, how I build, and how I love. Every day I make choices grounded in their values. In my professional life, I lead with integrity, advocate for fairness, and mentor others with the calm strength of Granny's tough love and the grace of my mom's example. In my personal life, I protect my peace, honor my words, and cherish my family. In my spiritual life, I remain anchored in prayer, living the scriptures they embodied more than quoted. Their wisdom also fuels my work as an attorney and educator. They taught me that wealth without wisdom is fragile, and that true stewardship of money, time, and truth is sacred. When I teach estate planning or financial literacy, I'm not just sharing professional knowledge; I'm carrying their blueprint forward.

Timeless Wisdom for A Modern Life

My mom once told me, "Dee, you need to write your book. You've got information to share." That was the moment the seed for this book truly took root. A quiet conviction settled in my spirit: Their lessons cannot die with them. This book is not written from pride, but from purpose. Not to boast about blessings, but to honor the inheritance of wisdom that sustained three generations of women who loved God, lived fully, and lifted others.

As I turned the corner into the my 60th birthday, gratitude and reflection walked hand in hand. What gleams brightest in my memory are not the milestones or accomplishments, but the lessons; the way Granny turned envelopes into miracles, the way Grandma Mary turned sweat and sacrifice into land and legacy, and the way Mom turned compassion and determination into power and made love look effortless. Their lessons were not delivered in sermons or speeches, they were lived.

Their values became my compass. Their resilience, my armor. Their dreams, my blueprint. Their prayers, my covering. These women were more than Mothers, they were truth-tellers, protectors, mentors, and spiritual architects who built me from the inside out. They taught me that love requires strength, that giving never leaves you empty, and that faith is not something you hold, it is something that holds you.

Resilience in Adversity — Faith With Feet

Resilience was not a word my Mothers used; it was a rhythm they lived. Grandma Mary rose before dawn to clean homes and businesses for white families who rarely saw the brilliance in her eyes. She was even trusted with a key to the town bank to clean on the weekends. She was often transported to work by her husband, R.L. "Sonny" Little, one of her adult children, or occasionally picked up by an employer.

Mom once recalled during one of our vacations in Mississippi seeing Grandma Mary picked up by a white woman whose house she cleaned. The passenger seat sat empty, Grandma Mary was required to ride in the back.

That moment while quiet, humiliating, and unforgettable revealed the world she endured. Yet she never allowed indignity to define her. Every dollar she earned, every house she scrubbed, brought her closer to freedom. The goal was to own the eighty acres of land outright one day.

Granny carried that same resolve northward when she and her husband, Charles Sanders, whom I affectionately called PaPa, left Cairo, Illinois, for Chicago in search of opportunity. Together, they built a life founded on faith, partnership, and perseverance. When society said "no," Granny simply said, "Not yet."

Mom inherited that same flame and fanned it into power. She rose from an entry-level clerical position to become Executive Director of a major social-service agency, balancing motherhood, marriage, night school, and leadership with quiet determination. Their stories were never just about endurance. They were about progress with purpose. They didn't wait for doors to open, they built their own thresholds.

Faith as Foundation

If resilience was their rhythm, faith was their melody. They didn't pray because it was customary, they prayed because it was necessary. Grandma Mary leaned on prayer when bills stacked high and strength ran low, trusting God to help her make the Annual ballon payment at the end of the year on Mississippi soil she purchased. Granny prayed over her family before every meal, every trip, every tough conversation. Mom drew peace from scripture, even in her final days, resting in the same faith that had carried generations before her. From them I learned that prayer is not the last resort, it is the first step. Their faith didn't erase hardship; it gave them the grace to walk through it with dignity and hope.

Their faith made the impossible possible.

Planning With Purpose — Legacy by Design

Nothing my Mothers left behind was accidental; every blessing was planned.

Grandma Mary didn't just buy land. She divided it legally among her children before passing away, ensuring that no generation would ever fight over what she had earned through sacrifice. Granny and PaPa refused to let redlining block their dream. They purchased their Englewood home on a Land Contract, changing the direction of our family's story.

Mom followed their lead, purchasing her own home with intention and later investing in property after her father's passing, more than ten years after Granny's transition. The equity and example born from Grandma

Mary's Mississippi land and Granny's Chicago home gave my mother the foundation to create investments of her own. They proved that ownership is not about possession. Ownership of land is about preparation.

Education, faith, and stewardship were their tools; foresight was their strategy. They built not just for their time, but for ours.

This book is my tribute and offering to my Mothers. I begin by sharing their stories: the choices they made, the challenges they faced, the grace with which they carried burdens that would have broken others. From their lives come lessons on faith, family, finances, love, and legacy. Their voices still echo in mine. Their wisdom still guides my steps. And as I write, I understand more clearly: their legacy is not only something I inherited, it is something I am responsible for.

So I pass it on to you with love, reverence, and hope. For every woman and man who longs to hear their mother's voice again. For every daughter or son who never got to ask all the questions. For every person shaped by steady hands and didn't realize it until later, may the lessons of my Mothers remind you that you, too, come from strength. May they fill the quiet spaces of your heart, and may these lesson light your path just as they continue to illuminate mine. As you read, look for the Reflection Questions and a prayer to help guide you. Prayer before action, pause before responding, rushing, or worrying. Let faith set the pace. Release and Rest, do what you can faithfully, then stop.

Trust God to handle what your strength cannot.

Deadra

CONTENTS

PART I: MY FOUNDATION
IN STRENGTH

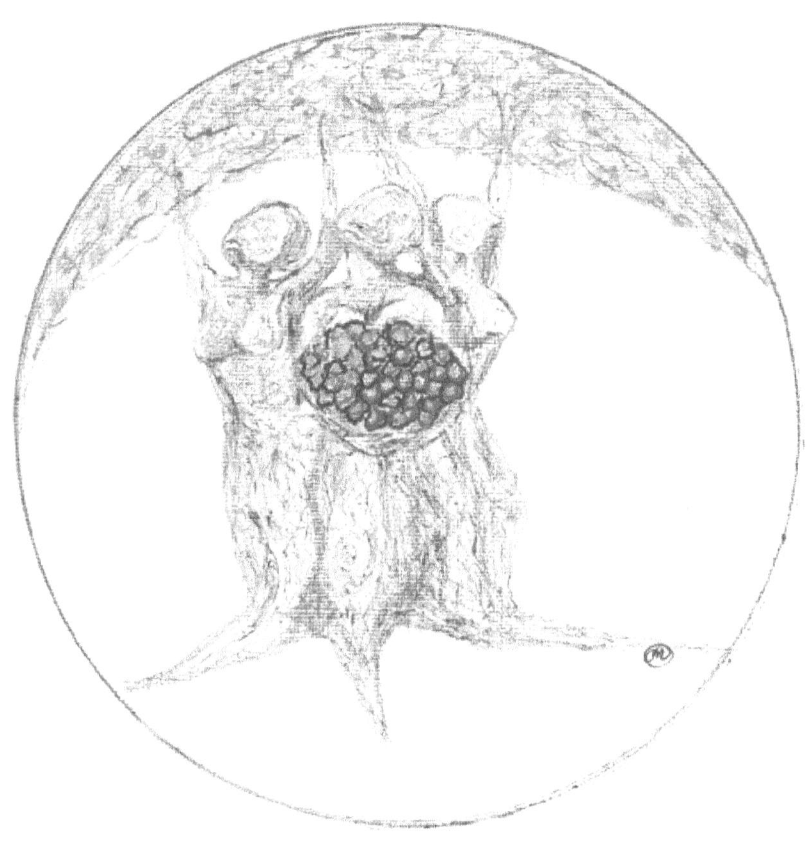

> *"She may have been five-foot-four, but in faith and vision, she stood among giants."*
> - Deadra W. Stokes

A GIANT IN SPIRIT, STEWARDSHIP, AND LEGACY

Though she measured barely five feet four, **Mary Nealy Little** filled every inch of her century with purpose. Born January 14, 1907, and blessed to live on this earth for 101 years, until October 15, 2008, Grandma Mary lived a life that turned labor into legacy. Her story is a masterclass in resilience, foresight, and the quiet authority of faith in action.

She did not simply raise a family, she built an inheritance of land and devotion that became both compass and currency for everyone who followed.

A Woman of Grace and Grit

Grandma Mary brought fourteen children into the world, including twins who passed at birth and another precious baby who was stillborn. She lovingly raised eleven through the hot, hard days of Scooba, Mississippi. In the Jim Crow South, opportunity was rationed and respect too often denied, yet she met each dawn with steady grace and prayer on her lips.

She was married twice, first to George Woods, whom my father was named after and later to R.L.

"Sonny" Little, her partner in both life and legacy. Together they built more than a household; they made a dream of reality.

My cousin Clara shared with me that when you stayed overnight at Grandma Mary's as a young child, you were expected to rise early in the morning to tend to the farm. Grandma never knocked on doors or shook anyone awake. She simply expected you to get up the way she did, early, quietly, and with purpose. On that farm, the day did not wait for you. The land did not wait for you. The work that had to be done did not wait for you. Grandma Mary understood what had to be done. She knew she had to tend to her crops and animals before she went off to clean the homes of many of her white employers. Before the sun rose, she had already watered plants, fed chickens, checked on the livestock, and walked the vast rows of her fields with intention. She was motivated not by money, but by mission. Her purpose was crystal-clear: to pay off the loan she secured to purchase those 80 acres, because she understood, in a way few did during her time, that land ownership was wealth, security, and legacy.

For decades, she worked tirelessly cleaning homes, churches, and the local bank, mopping marble floors, polishing brass fixtures, and sweeping long corridors for people who acknowledged her labor but rarely recognized her worth. She scrubbed, shined, dusted, and restored spaces that would never fully reflect the brilliance of the woman who maintained them.

Yet her integrity made her indispensable. She was entrusted with keys to private homes, to businesses, and even to the town bank to access after-hours and on weekends to clean. People may not have always valued her openly, but they trusted her with everything they had. Her honesty was her résumé and her reputation.

Grandma Mary worked hard, yes, But she was never driven solely by wages. She was working toward something far greater. She was working toward freedom. Toward ownership, security for her children, and a legacy that would stretch beyond her lifetime.

Everything she did, rising before dawn, tending to crops, cleaning other people's buildings, paying toward her mortgage multiple times a year was rooted in her unwavering belief that land was power, land was dignity, and land was the key to creating something that could not be taken away. Grandma Mary wasn't just building a farm; she was building a future.

The Dream of Land and Legacy

Long before it was fashionable to speak of "generational wealth," Grandma Mary envisioned it.

She did not want to rent. She did not want to depend. She wanted to own something earned by her own hands and sanctified by her own sacrifice.

During those times it was the tradition for land to get handed down to the male children to provide for their families. It was assumed that the female children would marry and their husbands would inherit land from their families and if not their husbands would secure land and/or a home for his wife and children. Grandma Mary knowing this secretly expressed to her cousin, Ola, her desire to own land. The story goes that Ola inherited a great deal of land from her deceased parents and after inheriting the land, she knew she needed to bless Grandma Mary with a chance of a lifetime.

Ola recognized the fire in Grandma Mary's eyes and when she inherited 160 acres of land she made a decision mixed with both faith and determination and decided that she would do something that would change the trajectory of an entire family. She offered her cousin a deal that was only for her and no one else: eighty acres at $100 per acre, less than half the price she would sale the land to the men in the family.

In 1967, Grandma Mary secured an FHA loan with payments of fifty dollars a month and an annual balloon note of one thousand fifty dollars. It was an overwhelming sum for a woman who earned her living cleaning homes, yet she faced it with the same quiet strength that had carried her through every storm. She cleaned more homes, accepted extra work, and carefully managed every dollar that both she and Mr. Sonny earned until the debt was fully paid.

Remarkably, she continued to rent the place where she lived while paying the mortgage on her newly acquired land. That sacrifice gave her the time she needed to build a small and modest home. In 1968, she and my grandfather, Mr. Sonny, completed construction of that home on the land she worked so hard to secure. It was a simple three-bedroom house, just enough space for Grandma Mary, Mr. Sonny, and her youngest daughter, my aunt Malree.

By taking every dollar that she and Mr. Sonny earned and saving it with purpose, Grandma Mary was able to make the final mortgage payment in 1981. Because she handled all of the household finances, Mr. Sonny had no idea what was coming when she proudly announced that the mortgage was paid in full. The note was stamped, "CANCELLED," and the deed bore their names, with the mortgage being fully released. But it was clear that God's fingerprints were all over it.

A Vision Beyond Ownership

Grandma Mary's genius was revealed not only in what she acquired, but in how thoughtfully she planned for the future. She had witnessed too many families lose what they worked so hard to build because of conflict and division, and she was determined that her children would not share that fate. In 1973, she hired an attorney and legally divided her eighty acres into ten equal parcels, one for each surviving child. Through that decision, she secured not only inheritance, but harmony. She was not merely passing down property; Grandma Mary was leaving her children peace of mind.

Today, that land still carries her name and her spirit. My youngest aunt, Malree, inherited the parcel with the modest three bedroom home, which is now her retirement residence. Unknown to Grandma Mary at the time, that very home would later become Malree's refuge when she was forced to flee New Orleans during Hurricane Katrina.

My aunt Ilet retired from her career as a registered nurse in Birmingham, Alabama, and returned to Scooba. There, she eventually built a beautiful and quaint retirement home on her portion of the land. My cousin Clara acquired her mother's share from her siblings and built her own retirement home on that parcel. Lastly, my beloved aunt Susie has allowed our family to use a portion of her land as a sacred burial ground. Grandma Mary, Mr. Sonny, two of my aunts, and my father, George Woods, are all laid to rest in this sacred soil.

It is the place where our roots run deep, where prayers rest beneath oak, pine, and pecan trees, and where Grandma Mary's voice still seems to travel on the Mississippi wind. That land is more than acreage. It is testimony and living proof of what happens when faith is joined with foresight.

A Century of Wisdom

Grandma Mary lived long enough to witness the harvest of every seed she planted. Her hands scrubbed floors, yet her mind laid foundations that would endure for generations. Her faith did not simply move mountains; it enabled her to acquire them. She was wise without formal schooling, strong without ever needing to raise her voice, and rich in ways that no amount of money could measure. She understood a truth that many never come to learn, that stewardship is sacred and ownership is power.

Her life reflected a form of leadership shaped not by titles, but by perseverance and purpose. It was rooted in the belief that what you build should endure, and that legacy is something created with intention.

The Lesson She Left Me

As I walk through my own sixties, I see her more clearly than ever. Her lessons have aged into revelation. She taught me that faith is active, not abstract, recorded in check stubs, lived in calloused hands, and measured in disciplined budgets. She showed me that legacy isn't what you leave, it's what you build while you're here. Whenever I stand on that Mississippi land, I feel her near. The red clay underfoot, the hush of wind through the trees, it all sounds like Grandma Mary whispering, "Give first. Work hard. Own something. Leave peace behind."

Grandma Mary Nealy Little was a steward, a strategist, and a spiritual warrior. She may have stood five-foot-four, but to those who knew her, and to generations yet unborn, she remains a giant in spirit, in stewardship, and in legacy.

*"Some women whisper wisdom into your ear.
Granny spoke it through the way she lived."*

- Deadra W. Stokes

MY EVERYTHING: GRACE UNDER PRESSURE

To the world, she was **Juanita Love Sanders**.

To our family, she was the backbone. To me, she was simply "Granny" and she was my everything. I was her only grandchild, my mother's only child, and the bond we shared was sacred, a love both gentle and unbreakable. She adored me completely, and I cherished her with every fiber of my being. From my earliest memories, I was always by her side. We even had birthdays one day apart, mine on December 30th and her on the 31st!

Because my mother worked full-time, pursued her degrees in the evenings, and styled hair on weekends, while my father worked long hours at the steel mill, Granny and my grandfather whom I lovingly called, "Papa" (pronounced Paw-Paw) became my world. Their large two-story home nestled in Englewood with a wraparound porch, wasn't just a place I stayed; it was the place where I was raised.

Adventures by Bus and by Faith

Ironically, Granny never learned to drive, and I truly believe she had no desire to do so. She seemed to delight in being chauffeured around town by either Papa or my mother. As a little girl, Granny and I shared a cherished Saturday early afternoon routine. We would walk a few blocks to 63rd Street to catch the bus headed west toward Halsted Street. There, we would spend the afternoon in what was then one of the busiest shopping corridors in Chicago's Black community.

We'd browse the aisles of major Department Stores, such as Sears and Goldblatt's. And sometimes we would shop in the many other stores that lined the corridor. Our day always ended the same way, arms full of bags, hearts full of joy, and lunch at the Walgreens Eat-In Diner. I can still smell the hamburgers sizzling on the flat grill, hear the jingle of bus fare, and see her soft smile across the booth. That was our rhythm, our Saturday ritual. Those trips were more than errands; they were acts of love disguised as routine. They grounded me. They gave me joy. And in the small spaces between laughter and lunch, Granny dropped the kind of wisdom that stitched itself into my soul.

Granny was diabetic and dealt with several health challenges, but she never let them define her. Instead, she turned even her illness into a lesson in readiness and responsibility. She made sure I knew her medications, where to find them in her purse, and what to do if her blood sugar ever dropped too low. "If I look a little dizzy," she'd say with a wink, "just hand me a peppermint." It never felt heavy or frightening, it felt like trust. At a young age, I learned what responsibility looked like. I carried it as a badge of honor. Deep down, I understood the assignment: if Granny couldn't handle it, I could.

Strength in Stillness

Granny stood just five feet three with her cafe au lait unblemished complexion, but her presence filled every room she entered. Born in Cairo, Illinois, one of four siblings, she carried strength in her stillness, the kind that doesn't demand attention but commands it anyway.

In 1941, she married Charles Sanders, my Papa, and together they built a life in Chicago rooted in faith, discipline, and quiet dignity. Granny's love was steady, but it wasn't soft. Her love required accountability, respect, restraint, and reverence. Family members often sent their children to stay with her when they needed "a little straightening out."

A few weeks at Granny's house could reset even the most stubborn spirit. She never needed to shout. Her calm was her power. Her silence was her sermon. She didn't raise her voice. She raised expectations.

With just one look, she could stop chaos in its tracks, not through fear, but through fortitude. She restored order without ever breaking peace.

A Quiet Revolutionary

Granny was a nurturer, and a visionary; a quiet revolutionary before the world had language for women like her. Long before "generational wealth" became a movement, she understood it. She believed that homeownership wasn't just about shelter, it was about dignity and self-determination. For Black families in the 1950s, that dream was often denied. Redlining and discrimination closed the doors of most banks.

Granny didn't believe in impossible. She believed in God's provision and her own persistence. When my grandfather and his brothers migrated one at a time from Alabama to Chicago, they collectively lived in one home.

My mother would share the many stories and memories she had sharing a home with her three uncles and their families. Despite being an only child she never felt alone because she grew up in the home with her cousins. Each family worked together to save their money independently to secure their own home. One by one, my grandfather and his brothers each located their respective family homes. They utilized creative financing before creative financing was called "creative financing" because back then securing a mortgage as an African American was not easily done. In most instances, we had to trust and acquire home ownership creatively.

Through faith and grit, Papa and my Granny found a path through a man I recall them referring to as Mr. Clancy. Thanks to him, the doors to homeownership opened. I would later discover that Mr. Clancy, a Caucasian man, agreed to sell them a home on what is referred to commonly as a Land Contract. In most states, including Illinois, it is referred to as an Installment Agreement for Deed. This option allowed homebuyers an opportunity to purchase by bypassing banks that often said no.

I recall riding in the back seat while my grandfather picked my Grandmother up from work on Fridays. She would hand him an envelope with money in it and we would drive to Mr. Clancy's home. I would see Papa get out of the car and hand him the envelope.

While I was not there to witness the tendering of the final payment, I did learn that a day came when Granny and Papa made their final payment to Mr. Clancy and owned their property outright.

That final payment closed the chapter on struggle and opened the door to ownership, it was the moment that their home become theirs through dedication and determination. The day they paid Mr. Clancy in full was the day my grandparents broke a barrier that banks tried to build around them.

Brick by Brick, Blessing by Blessing

While both my Papa and Granny worked together, it was Granny who created the budget, separated payments for bills in envelopes, wrote her budget on envelopes to make certain that every bill was paid with what both her and Papa had earned.

Each wall whispered the truth that faith and discipline, paired with patience and prayer, can accomplish what others call impossible. Every bill paid was a testimony. Every sacrifice, a seed. Granny and Papa built more than a house, they built a foundation for our family's identity. A declaration that Black perseverance is not mere survival…it is creation.

While at one time the house was a single family home, it had been divided into two separate living quarters for two households, one living on the first floor and the other living on the second floor. Papa and Granny occupied the entire first floor and over time the second floor would be the home to numerous family members. It was a safe haven, a place where people could land on their feet during transition. That home in Englewood stood as proof that when a woman builds in faith, her work echoes for generations.

It was that home, the one they purchased brick by brick, blessing by blessing, that later gave my mother, Barbara Jean Woods, her own foundation. After my grandfather's passing, more than ten years after Granny transitioned, that property allowed my mother to begin investing in real estate and creating wealth of her own.

Granny and Papa's dedication did not just give their only child a roof over her head, it gave her a roadmap. Their faith made ownership possible, and their discipline made prosperity inevitable.

Grace That Carried Generations

To me, Granny was everything a child could need. She was my guardian, teacher, compass, and sanctuary. Her lessons never came through lectures. They came while she hummed hymns in the kitchen, baked her golden pound cake, or sat on the porch during humid Chicago summers, laughing and sharing stories.

She bragged about me to anyone who would listen, convinced me that I could do anything and because she believed it, so did I. It was nothing for Granny to embarrass me when speaking of my achievements to anyone who would listen. The belief she had in me; the words she loudly expressed in my presence and the faith she had in me became my first inheritance. I often wish my daughters could have known her, to feel her quiet confidence, to witness her unshakeable calm, to taste her love baked into every slice of that pound cake.

Even now, she's with me. When I'm uncertain, I hear her voice: "You already know what to do, trust yourself." When I'm weary, I see her face, providing me wisdom and guidance. Granny showed me that love is work, that patience is power, and that legacy is built on choices, not chances. Every time I keep my word, extend grace instead of judgment, or lift my chin and walk in faith I honor her.

Juanita Love Sanders was a woman of few words but infinite influence. Her faith steadied our family. Her vision anchored our future. Her love made me whole. Through her life, I learned that grace under pressure doesn't just endure, it transforms everything it touches.

MY MOTHER, MY HERO

On February 4, 2022, just six weeks after being diagnosed with stage IV gallbladder cancer, my beloved mother, **Barbara Jean Woods**, or "Mom Barb" as so many affectionately called her, took her final flight home.

Even now, there are no words strong enough to capture the magnitude of her loss or the depth of her love. She was my everything, my foundation, my fiercest protector, and truly, the wind beneath my wings.

I was her only child, but she made sure I never felt like anything was missing. If I dreamed it, she found a way to make it possible. If I needed it, it appeared before I could ask. She poured every ounce of herself into ensuring my life was filled with opportunity, joy, and stability. She didn't just provide what I needed, she often gave me what I didn't even know I wanted. Always anticipating. Always giving. Always loving.

Everyone's Mom

In high school, she wasn't just my mom, she became everyone's mom to those who knew her. Whether we were headed to a party or coming home late, she was there. She would pick up my friends and I in the middle of the night, drive across the city, and make sure they got home safely, even if that meant going miles past our own neighborhood.

When I asked why, she'd simply say, "I could never forgive myself if something happened to one of your friends and I hadn't offered to bring them home."

That was the kind of mother she was…selfless, watchful, and unshakably devoted to the safety of those she loved. But it didn't stop with my friends. As I grew older, I began to realize that her love stretched far beyond our family circle. Former coworkers, church members, neighbors, even strangers would later tell me stories of how "Mom Barb" had quietly mentored, encouraged, or comforted them when they needed it most. She didn't need recognition. She just needed to help. That was her ministry, the quiet kind, delivered through kindness, consistency, and care.

Grace and Greatness in Every Role

Professionally, my mother was the embodiment of excellence and grace. The only child of Charles and Juanita Sanders, she married young, just twenty-one, but never allowed her circumstances to define her ceiling. While working full-time as a Corporate Executive Assistant, she returned to school, earning both her bachelor's and master's degrees through sheer determination.

Her career began in social work and grew into leadership. She rose through the ranks at Ada S. McKinley and eventually became Executive Director, leading with equal parts strength and compassion. Her colleagues respected her and her staff adored her. Those who worked for her often said the same thing, "She expected your best, because she always gave hers." When she retired, Mom didn't slow down. She joined me in my law firm, lending her professionalism and warmth to our clients and staff. Before long, everyone from my office staff, interns, along with clients in my office started calling her "Mom Barb." And she smiled every time she heard it. Because that's who she was, a mother to many, not just by birth, but by heart.

The Power of Independence

During my high school years, we lived in Hyde Park, in a beautiful high-rise with all of the urban luxuries: a doorman, underground parking, and a fitness club. Life felt safe, comfortable, and bright. But after her divorce, my mother decided that renting was not our final destination. She believed deeply in homeownership, not as a financial move, but as a declaration of independence and stability.

I'll never forget the day she found her first home. A retiring developer was offering new townhomes on land he had quietly held for decades. The reservation deposit was just $100. Without hesitation, I watched my mother step forward, her confidence radiating, and place the deposit down. That home became hers, a symbol of perseverance and self-reliance.

The Wind Beneath My Wings

Now, as I reflect, I see so clearly that so much of who I am is because of who she was. Her discipline became my structure. Her laughter became my joy. Her prayers became my protection. There isn't a day that passes when I don't feel her presence, when I don't hear her voice urging me to "keep pushing," or sense her pride when I help someone the way she would have. She may have left this earth, but she will never leave my life.

*"Some people give you life.
My mother gave me flight."*
- Deadra W. Stokes

Her Legacy In Me

My mother taught me that strength doesn't have to be loud, that kindness doesn't make you weak, and that success is sweetest when it empowers others.

Every student I mentor, every client I encourage, every young person I remind of their worth, that's my mother's voice echoing through mine. Barbara Jean Woods didn't just raise me. She raised a standard. She raised a legacy. She raised a life that continues to honor her. She was and always will be my hero, my anchor, and the wind that carried me higher than I could ever have flown alone. And so I live with gratitude. Because I was and always will be Barbara Jean Woods's daughter.

PART II: TIMELESS WISDOM

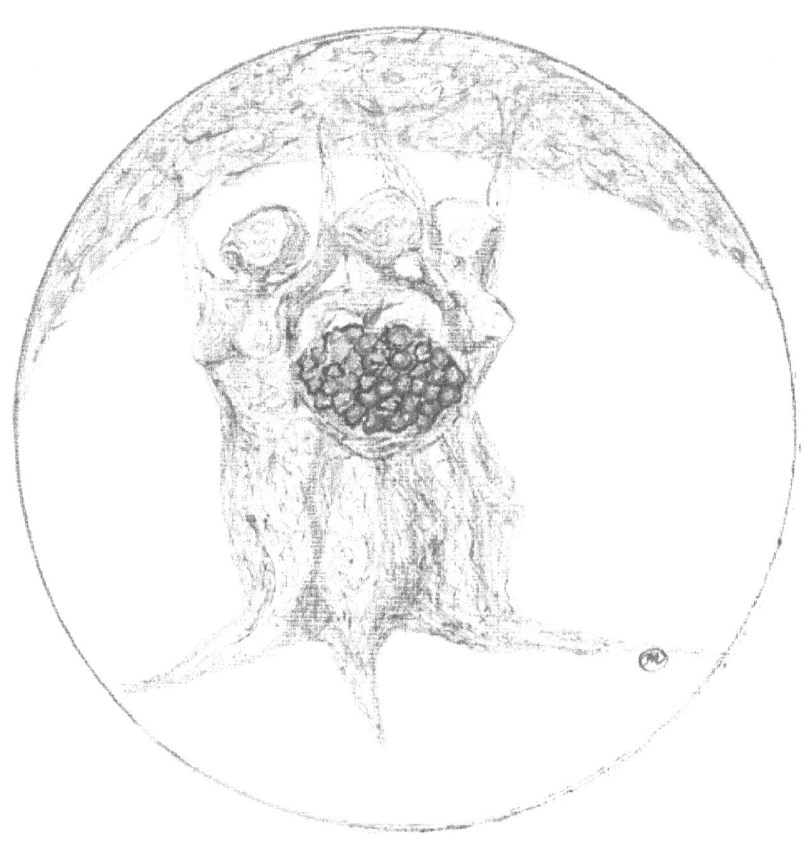

AN INVITATION

Some books do not simply arrive, they are summoned. *Timeless* is such a book.

It carries the weight of lived truth, the rhythm of ancestral memory, and the quiet authority of wisdom earned over time. Long before these lessons were named, they were embodied. Long before they were gathered onto the page, they were practiced in kitchens and sanctuaries, in whispered prayers and disciplined choices, in love that corrected and faith that endured.

To read this book is to step into lineage.

Black women are not only bearers of children; we are bearers of history. We are descendants of women whose bodies traveled the Middle Passage. Some endured the ships, holding language, prayer, and memory inside of themselves, and others who refused captivity so completely that they entrusted their bodies to the waters rather than to chains. Both were acts of resistance. Both were declarations of worth. Both mothered generations they would never see. Their courage did not disappear into the ocean—it echoes in us.

We are our ancestors' survival made visible. We carry their wisdom at the cellular level—lessons etched into our DNA, teaching our bodies how to endure, our spirits how to adapt, and our souls how to hope long before we ever find the language for survival. Scripture names this sacred continuity, reminding us that "we are surrounded by so great a cloud of witnesses" (Hebrews 12:1), urging us forward with strength borrowed from those who ran before us.

That ancestral strength finds expression in the life of my friend and Soror, Deadra Woods Stokes. Her steadiness, her discernment, her unapologetic faith—these are not accidental traits. They are inherited. They were shaped by women who understood that legacy is not about recognition, but responsibility.

Chief among them was her mother, Barbara J. Woods—a woman whose faith was practiced more than proclaimed, whose life taught that service is not an obligation but a calling. She mothered with intention, lived with an open hand, and left behind not noise, but a way. Her presence still teaches. Her example still guides.

The wisdom of this book also reaches further back to her grandmothers, Mary Nealy Little and Juanita Love Sanders, women shaped by endurance, prayer, and quiet courage. Their resilience lives between these pages, reminding us that some lessons are passed down not in words, but in ways of surviving, loving, and believing.

As I honor these women, I must also honor my own mother, Harriet Edwards, who taught me lessons that live in my bones. She showed me how to stand—how to speak truth even when my voice trembled, how to hold faith when answers were delayed, how to love without losing myself. Harriet Edwards taught me that strength and softness are not opposites, and that obedience to God often requires courage long before it brings clarity. Through her, I learned that mothering—and mentoring—is an act of daily resistance in a world that underestimates Black women's wisdom.

Together, these women—along with aunties, church mothers, mentors, and spiritual elders—form a sacred circle of instruction. They remind us that no one is self-made. We are community-made. Prayer-covered. Legacy-shaped. As the Psalmist declares, "One generation shall commend your works to another, and shall declare your mighty acts" (Psalm 145:4).

Timeless is the fruit of that covering. The 22 lessons offered here are not abstractions. They are distilled truth—seasoned by scripture, sharpened by experience, and softened by grace. In their intentionality, structure, and spirit, they stand as a quiet homage to the 22 visionary women who founded Delta Sigma Theta Sorority, Incorporated—women who believed in scholarship, service, sisterhood, and social responsibility. Like those founders, these lessons call us to live faithfully, think critically, serve boldly, and love expansively.

Legacy, as these pages so beautifully affirm, is not what we leave behind. It is what we live out daily. It is how we honor the prayers of those who came before us and prepare the ground for those who will follow.

I am grateful that Deadra Woods Stokes said yes to the assignment of this book. Her obedience ensures that wisdom forged in the lives of faithful Black women will continue to speak, guide, and bless.

May these pages remind you who you come from. May they steady you in who you are becoming. And may they call you to live in such a way that your life—and the lives that shaped you—bear fruit for generations, fulfilling the promise that "their descendants shall be known among the nations" (Isaiah 61:9), and that your living, loving, and leading will indeed be timeless.

Rev. Dr. Stacey Edwards-Dunn

Trinity United Church of Christ, Executive Pastor

FAITH & FOUNDATIONS

"But seek ye first the kingdom of God, and His
righteousness; and all these things shall
be added unto you."

— Matthew 6:33 (KJV)

TIMELESS

22 LESSONS OF FAITH, HOPE & LOVE

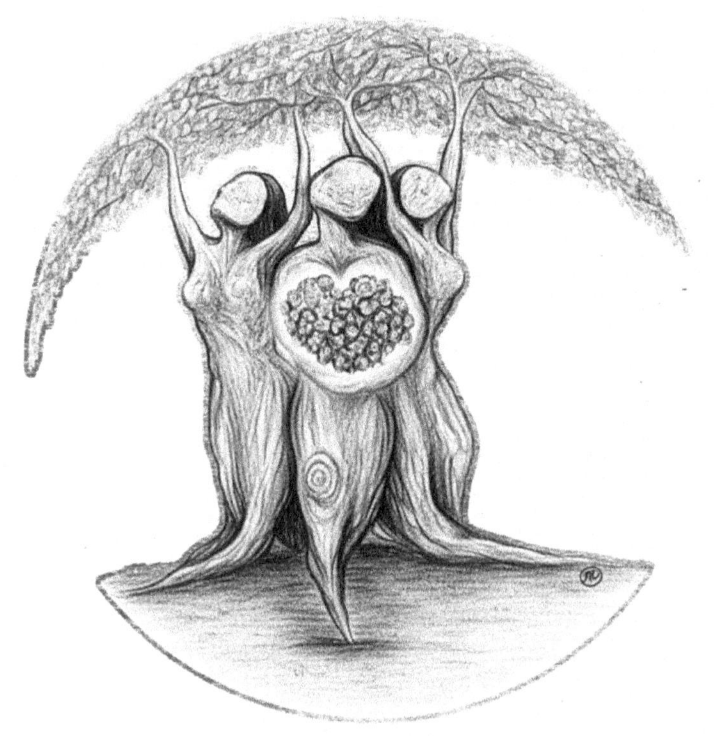

*"Do all that you can —
then put the rest in God's hands."*

\- Barbara J. Woods

1 - FAITH IS A LIFELINE, NOT A LAST RESORT

Faith is where everything began.

Long before I understood the power of prayer, I saw it lived out daily by the three women who became the blueprint of my becoming: Grandma Mary, Granny, and my Mom. They weren't the same in background, education, or lifestyle, yet they were rooted in the same truth: They didn't just believe in God. They depended on God. Where the world told them to strive harder, they chose to seek God first. Faith wasn't their backup plan, it was their guiding strategy.

Faith in the Field

With only a grade-school education and more hard days than easy ones, Grandma Mary understood faith not as a concept but as a necessity. She prayed seeds into the ground. She prayed food onto the table. She prayed strength into her bones after long days. Her faith made land fruitful. Her faith made lack look like abundance. She believed that God was the source and that everything else was simply a resource.

Faith in Education & Service

Granny returned to school when I was a young girl and obtained her associate's degree in early childhood education. Shortly after graduating, she would become the Director of our Church's Nursery School Program. She poured her love and compassion into the children and families who came through the doors of that nursery school. She used her special gift of giving and showing love to serve others, especially children and close family.

She taught that your calling is shaped by what God placed inside you, not by the limitations of others. Her prayers often sounded like purpose, focused, bold, and full of expectation.

Faith in Family & Forward Motion

My Mother lived her faith through action, always pushing forward, trusting God's timing, always making a way out of no way. She often reminded me, "Do all that you can, then put the rest in God's hands." She literally prayed over everything, her family, over decisions, over bills, over futures. Her faith was not just a shield and a shovel, it was both protection and progress.

One Lesson, Lived Three Ways

Their expressions of faith were distinct but unified. Their devotion wasn't loud or performative. It was steady. Daily. Practical.

Faith showed up in: Morning prayers over the day's work; Quiet conversations with God while doing ordinary tasks; Nighttime gratitude no matter what the day held. Faith wasn't what they ran to when trouble came. Faith was what kept trouble from breaking them.

What They Taught Me

From their example, I learned that faith is anchored in three truths: 1.) Pray before reacting, 2.) Trust God when answers are unclear; and 3.) Believe that if God gave you the vision, He will certainly give you the provision.

Seeking God first isn't an event. It's a posture, a lifestyle, and a lifeline.

Life Application

Faith is not the last option. It is the first instruction. Seeking God first means:

- Invite God into every decision and pray before you take the first step;

- Trust that God's plan is bigger than your fear

- Believe that if you have the Vision, God will provide the path.

- Let go of control and embrace divine alignment knowing that God's path is not the one you may envision.

When God is first, everything else finds its rightful place. Because when you truly seek God first, you don't just survive the storm, you find strength, clarity, and even joy right in the rain. Ask yourself, *"Have I invited God into this?"*

REFLECTION

Identify one need, decision, or dream.

____

____

____

____

Three ways I can see that God has showed up in my life:

____

____

____

____

Identify something in my life that I need to let go and allow God to guide me.

____

____

____

____

PRAYER

God,

Guide my words, thoughts, and steps today.

Amen.

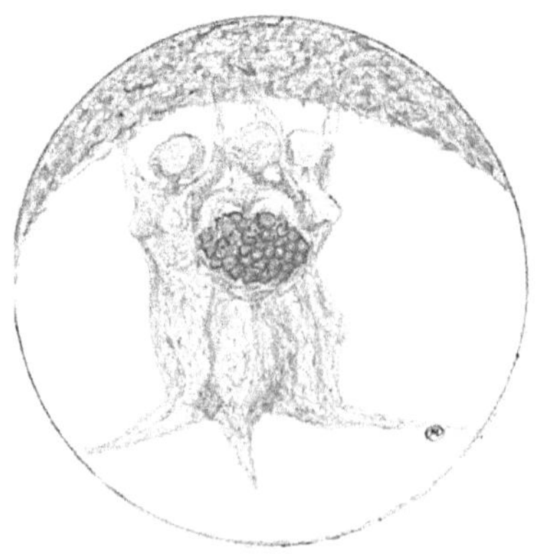

2 - STEWARDSHIP AS A CALLING

In each of both of my grandmothers as well as my own mother's homes giving was not an occasional gesture, it was a spiritual rhythm, a visible expression of gratitude to God. Stewardship wasn't just a doctrine preached on Sunday; it was a lifestyle lived Monday through Saturday.

In the Black Baptist tradition, giving back to God was expected and esteemed. We do not refer to it as generosity, it is called Tithing. It was the recognition that everything we have comes from God, and returning a portion to God keeps us humble, grateful, and aligned with God's purpose.

Faith in Action — The Open Hand

Giving was never optional in my upbringing. It was a way of life modeled by my Mothers and taught through their daily actions. As far back as I can remember, their hands were always open. They gave to the church, to family, to friends, and to those whose need was seen and unseen. They understood that abundance moves through generosity, and that blessings cannot rest in hands unwilling to release what they hold.

Their generosity was not born of excess or convenience. It was born of faith. They believed that giving was an expression of trust in God, a declaration that provision would come even when resources felt limited. What they offered was often sacrificial, yet it was always intentional and rooted in obedience.

Aside for giving and supporting their respective church, they also taught that stewardship extended beyond the walls of the church. Giving can take many forms — supporting community organizations, helping someone in need, offering time, resources, or encouragement. Stewardship, in its truest sense, is about recognizing that everything we have is a gift from God, and that we are called to use it with open hands and faithful hearts.

Grandma Mary — Giving from the Ground Up

I begin with my Grandma Mary, whose life in Scooba, Mississippi, was a living sermon on giving. Despite having fourteen children and more grandchildren than one could count, she somehow managed to provide for everyone and still had enough left to share.

When you visited Grandma Mary, you never left empty-handed. She would send you home with bags of fresh vegetables from her farm: collard greens, peas, beans, corn, and whatever else grew in her fields that season. She fed her children, grandchildren, neighbors, and anyone who found their way to her doorstep.

She didn't just feed bodies, she fed spirits. Her giving was an act of worship, a living tithe. And even when times were lean, Grandma Mary trusted that what she gave would come back multiplied. She lived out Malachi 3:10 before I knew the scripture by heart. Her faith, like her fields, produced a harvest that blessed generations.

"Bring the whole tithe into the storehouse, that there may be food in my house. Test me in this," says the Lord Almighty, "and see if I will not throw open the floodgates of heaven and pour out so much blessing that there will not be room enough to store it."

— Malachi 3:10 (NIV)

Granny — The Miracle Worker of Money

Then there was my Granny, the miracle worker when it came to finances. Granny could stretch a dollar further than anyone I've ever known. She had an uncanny ability to balance a budget on a shoestring and make it work.

I remember watching my mother drive her to one of her sisters' homes so she could drop off funds to help them make ends meet. If one of her nieces or nephews lost their way, Granny didn't just pray for them, she took them in, fed them, disciplined them, and sent them back out better than she found them.

Her giving wasn't just financial; it was corrective, compassionate, and consistent. She believed that money was meant to move, to circulate blessings, not collect dust. And even when she gave what little she had, she would smile and say, "God always makes a way, out of no way." For Granny, stewardship meant using every resource, time, talent, or treasure to uplift others and honor God.

Mom — Giving Through Service

Then, there was Mom, the heart of service personified. A licensed clinical social worker by profession. By purpose, she spent much of her career as an Executive Director of Special Education School, counseling and helping people families manage children who were differently able while experiencing some of life's hardest challenges. Her giving wasn't always public or formal; it was quiet, private, and deeply personal.

After she retired, she worked part-time for me in my law firm. Many days, as I walked past her office which was tucked away in a corner of my office, I would see one of my employees sitting across from her talking softly, sometimes even shedding a tear. I never asked what was said between them, and she never told me. What they shared stayed between them. I was always aware that her presence was a blessing, to me and to everyone she encountered. She continued to minister, to counsel, and comfort, just in a different setting.

That was who she was, selfless, thoughtful, and giving to her core. Her kindness wasn't conditional; it was instinctual. She didn't just talk about compassion, she practiced it in motion, one conversation, one quiet act of care at a time.

Mom's legacy was one of service through presence. Whether she was leading an organization, offering a listening ear, or ensuring a teenager got home safely, she gave of herself fully. Her open hand and open heart made her life a living testimony to what it means to be a cheerful giver.

The Collective Lesson: Giving Is a Lifestyle

From Grandma Mary's farm in Mississippi to Granny's budgeting table in Chicago to Mom's counseling sessions with those in need, my Mothers all shared one truth: You can't out-give God. They didn't give because it was easy; they gave because it was right.

They didn't give to be seen; they gave to serve. And every single time, God provided.

They taught me that when you release what's in your hand, God releases what's in His. That is the rhythm of divine exchange and the reason why a closed hand never gets fed.

Over the years, I've learned that giving whether it's tithing, serving, or encouraging someone, is one of the most powerful acts of faith. When you give the first ten percent, you declare that you trust God to make the ninety percent stretch further than a hundred ever could. And He does.

Doors open, opportunities appear, and peace replaces panic, but stewardship doesn't stop at the offering plate. It extends to how you spend your time, how you share your talents, and how you use your voice to uplift others. Giving back, whether to your church, community, or a cause that uplifts someone else, is your investment in the kind of world you want to live in. When you give, you participate in God's economy, one that never crashes, never defaults, and always yields a return. The return may not come as cash or credit, but it will show up in peace, provision, and purpose.

My Mothers lives proved that when you tithe, when you give, when you live with open hands, you don't lose anything, you make room for more. That's the essence of stewardship: trusting that everything you release returns multiplied, pressed down, and running over. Giving isn't about loss, it is about being in alignment. It's how you keep your heart and your blessings in rhythm with God. Everything belongs to God. We are managers, not owners, of the resources God places in our hands.

Life Application

1. **Honor God with Your First Fruits.** - Commit to giving God your first ten percent, not what is left over. Tithing is an act of trust that keeps God at the center of your priorities.

2. **Live Generously and Intentionally.** Identify one person, organization, or cause you can bless this week. Give from the heart, remembering that generosity creates space for God to move and replenish what is released.

3. **Steward More Than Money.** Offer your time, talents, and gifts in service to your church or community. Stewardship extends beyond finances and includes compassion, skills, and influence.

4. **Practice Quiet Kindness and Watch God Work.** Perform acts of kindness without seeking recognition. Pay attention to how God restores, provides, and multiplies what you give.

REFLECTION

What do my choices with time, money, and energy reveal about what I value most?

____

____

____

____

____

How can I give more intentionally this season?

____

____

____

____

How am I using my time, talents and kindness to serve others without seeking recognition?

____

____

____

____

PRAYER

God,

God, help me to trust You with all that has been placed in my care. Teach me to give generously, live with an open hand, and steward my time, gifts, and resources with faith and purpose. Guide my heart to serve quietly and faithfully, trusting You to provide and multiply what is given.

Amen.

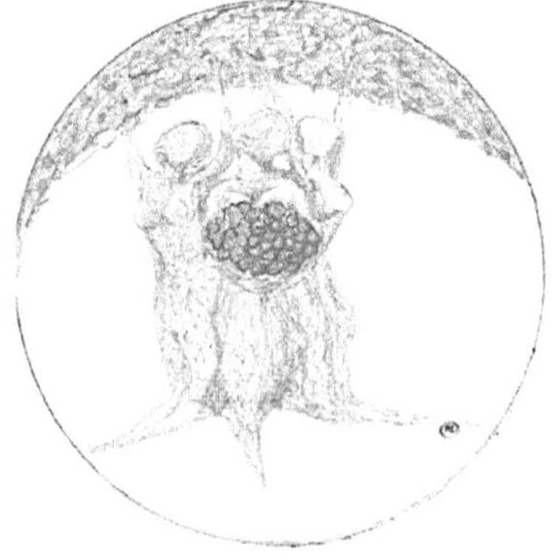

3 - IF THERE IS A WILL, THERE IS A WAY

My Mothers carried a quiet but powerful faith that guided every step of their lives. They believed deeply that what the mind could envision, faith could pursue. Nothing was dismissed as impossible simply because the path was unclear. Faith, they taught me, is not about knowing every step in advance. It is about trusting that the steps will appear once you begin to move.

My Aunt Malree once shared that one of Grandma Mary's favorite sayings was, "If there is a will, there is a way." It was her way of reminding us that desire, when paired with faith, always creates possibility. Sometimes the way forward is not immediately visible. That is where faith becomes the guide. You do all that you can, and then you trust faith to carry you farther than your sight ever could.

Grandma Mary: Believing Before Receiving

When Grandma Mary first dreamed of owning land where she could build a home for her children and family, she had no idea how that dream would come to pass. She did not have a blueprint or a guarantee. What she did have was determination, a willingness to work hard, and faith that opportunity would meet preparation. She shared her desire with her cousin Ola, someone she trusted and someone who wouldn't diminish her dream. Grandma Mary was not asking for a handout or special treatment. She spoke her vision out loud to someone who understood the value of land and legacy. That conversation became the doorway to the opportunity she had been praying for. What once felt distant became real. Grandma Mary trusted that if God placed the vision in her heart, provision would follow. She believed long before she received, and faith met her obedience.

Granny: Making a Little Become Enough

Everyone turned to Granny when they needed help, but I was her only grandchild, and I had a front-row seat to her wisdom. Many assumed she must have earned a great deal of money, yet the truth was far simpler. Granny understood stewardship. She knew how to save, plan, and make every dollar matter.

I remember when banks offered Christmas Savings Clubs. Starting in January, you would deposit a small amount each week, and by Thanksgiving you had enough to prepare for the holidays. Granny believed in systems like that, but she also created her own. She saved money in the bank, and she tucked bills into cans she had carefully prepared with small slits. I watched her fold each dollar and slide it away with intention.

There were days when she would invite me to help open the cans. I was always amazed by how much she had saved and even more amazed that no one in the household ever felt the absence of the money she had set aside. From her, I learned that discipline does not feel like deprivation when it is guided by purpose.

When family members came to Granny with a need, I watched her listen carefully and then help them chart a path forward. She wrote plans and numbers on envelopes, and what she wrote down almost always came to life. Granny lived the wisdom of Habakkuk 2:2, "Write the vision and make it plain." She understood that clarity invites movement and that movement makes room for provision.

Grace That Never Stopped Moving

My mother was determination wrapped in grace.

I remember attending college classes with her while I was still a child. After work, she would pick me up from school, we would grab something to eat, and then head to her evening classes. Sometimes I sat beside her in the classroom. Other times I sat in the library doing homework while she attended classes. That is where my love for libraries began.

When she completed one degree, she simply set her sights on the next. Doubt never entered the room. She trusted that if the desire was planted within her, a way would open. She seized opportunity when it appeared and never questioned whether she belonged in the space she worked so hard to enter.

The Power of Consistency

My Mothers never sought quick success. They understood that real triumphs are born in unseen hours. Early mornings, late nights and small sacrifices all add up to something sacred. They worked when they were tired and when no one thanked them. They worked because they believed in something greater than themselves. My Mothers taught me that dreams without discipline are just wishes. If you want something, study for it. Save for it. Sacrifice for it. When you finally reach it, keep working to honor the journey and make the way smoother for those who follow.

The Legacy of Labor

Now I understand what they always knew. There are no shortcuts to a meaningful life. The road requires effort, patience, and persistence. The women who raised me never asked for ease. They asked for opportunity, and when it arrived, they showed up ready to work.

That is the legacy I carry forward. It is the lesson I share with my students, my children, and my community. I do not fear hard work because work shaped me. Faith gave me direction, and effort carried me forward. When there is a will rooted in purpose, a way will always unfold.

Life Application

- **Identify something meaningful you want to accomplish**. Then take a moment to consider the consistent actions that will move you closer to it.

- **Focus on progress, not speed.** Give yourself permission to begin, quietly, slowly, even imperfectly.

- **Keep moving forward, not because circumstances are ideal, but because the intention behind your effort matters.** Remind yourself: God honors movement, strengthens effort, and completes what you persevere toward.

REFLECTION

What is one meaningful goal on my heart, and what small step can I take toward it now?

____

____

____

____

What has been holding me back, and how can I move forward in faith?

____

____

____

____

In what area of my life is God nudging me to begin again?

____

____

____

____

PRAYER

God,

When my will aligns with Your purpose, a way will always appear.

Amen.

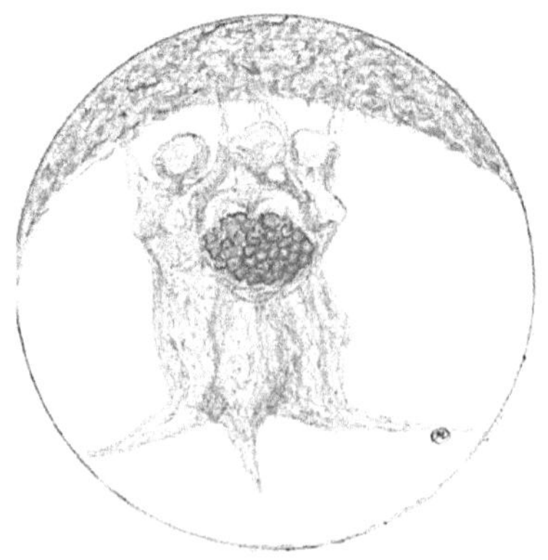

WEALTH, WORK, & WELLNESS

TIMELESS

22 LESSONS OF FAITH, HOPE & LOVE

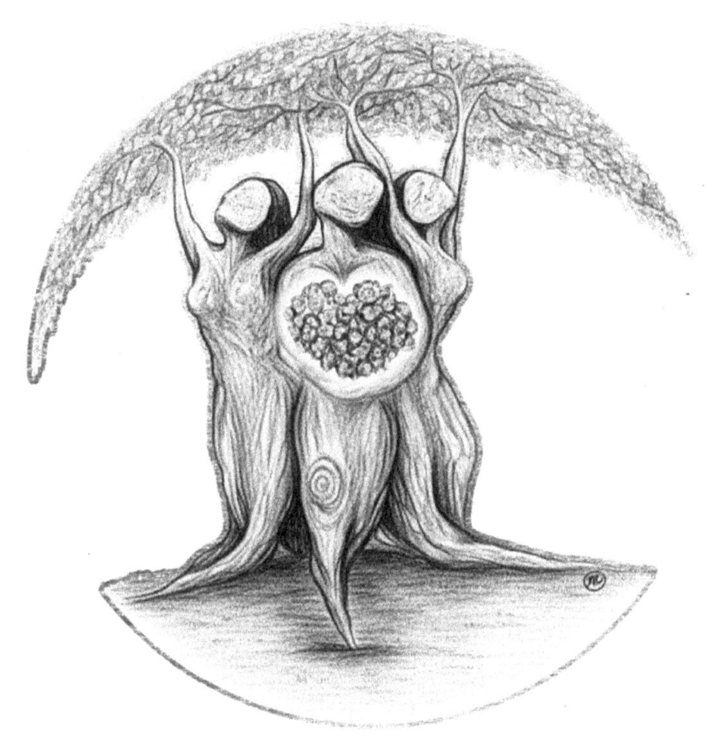

*"I want land
for my children!"*
- Grandma Mary

4 – LAND IS POWER, OWNERSHIP IS LEGACY

For my Mothers, land was not just dirt and deeds, it was destiny. It was proof that work had purpose, that a name carried value, and that sacrifice could outlive the person who made it. In their eyes, ownership was more than possession. It was protection. It was freedom. It was legacy. The women who raised me understood that the difference between struggle and stability often came down to one simple question: do you own something that cannot be taken from you?

The Seed of a Dream

"I want land for my children!" Those words were often whispered and sometimes spoken aloud by my Grandma Mary, as her youngest daughter, my Aunt Malree, remembers. Grandma Mary did not dream of acreage for prestige or pride. She wanted land so her children could inherit something lasting. Though she had no formal schooling beyond grammar school, she understood a truth far deeper than textbooks: land creates leverage, and ownership builds legacy.

We are sometimes taught to keep our desires to ourselves and guard them closely. But if Grandma Mary had never shared her desire with her cousin Ola, the opportunity that shaped our family might never have come. The lesson within the lesson is this: share your vision with people who can truly hold it. Choose those who will not be intimidated by it, threatened by it, or determined to shrink it. Aspirations that reach high can unsettle small thinking, so be selective and prayerful. But do not be silent.

Ola was the right person. She was not offended, jealous, or envious of Mary's goal. She was established and confident, a leader long before the word entered our everyday language, and she held 160 acres in her name.

When Ola heard Mary's heart, she responded with opportunity. She sold Mary eighty acres at a discount, not as charity but as stewardship. It was strong women lifting one another while keeping the transaction honorable. That discount was Ola's way of giving back, a living echo of Lesson Two, and it became a gift that continues to give. Today, those same acres support three retirement homes: two for my aunts and one for my cousin. This is what legacy looks like in real life.

In the red clay of Mississippi, Grandma Mary learned early that whoever owned the land owned the story. She watched others work from sunup to sundown on soil they did not own, always one step away from losing everything. She resolved to change that reality for her family.

Through endless days of labor, cleaning homes, cooking for others, and saving every spare dime that she and Mr. Sony earned, Grandma Mary invested not in things that fade but in land that endures. When she purchased her 80-acre farm, it was not just property. It was proof of perseverance. Those acres represented self-sufficiency, dignity, and the ability to feed not only her children but generations to come. Every fence post and row of crops spoke the same truth. The land was her offering to the future.

Grandma Mary's legacy taught me that land is sacred not because of what grows on it, but because of what it represents. It is the right to stand on ground that belongs to you.

Seeds of Ownership

In Chicago, Granny carried that Southern truth into city life. For her, ownership looked like a front porch, a spacious home that could welcome family in seasons of transition, and a place where Sunday dinners affirmed that she had arrived. She and my grandfather did not have much by the world's standards, yet in truth they had everything they wanted and more. They lived in a spacious home in Englewood on a quiet block, owned two cars they proudly called their own, and enjoyed a large half acre backyard that my grandfather carefully cultivated with fresh vegetables every spring and summer. In fact, Papa was known for having the greenest and most meticulously manicured lawn on the block.

What they had was paid for through prayer and budgets carefully written on the backs of white envelopes. I can still recall how Granny would take the very envelopes meant for bills and use the back to thoughtfully calculate her and Papa's budget. Like Grandma Mary, Granny's goal was for her and Papa to finish paying the land contract so they could own their Englewood home outright.

For my mother, ownership was never only about acquiring property. It was about sustaining what had been earned, protecting it with intention, and planning for what could one day be passed down. When my mother purchased her first piece of property, I remember speaking with the developer. He shared that the land where the townhome was built had been purchased by him at a tax sale twenty years earlier. For two decades, he paid only the nominal tax bill on vacant land before deciding to develop and construct the townhomes he was now selling. That history explained why he required only a one hundred dollar deposit to hold a new construction townhome. It is remarkable how God works, turning what once seemed almost impossible or unimaginable into reality.

Grandma Mary never gathered my Mothers around a table to give a formal lesson about land, yet the message echoed throughout their lives. Own something that lasts, or own something that helps build a legacy.

Life Application

- **Speak your vision to the right people**. Not everyone can carry your dream, so share it with those who will protect it rather than shrink it. Build with intention and practice stewardship along the way. Earning is only the beginning. Protecting what you acquire and preparing to pass it forward is how a blessing multiplies.

- **Adopt a practical playbook**. Start small and think long. Explore vacant lots, tax sale opportunities, or rural acreage. Modest holdings can grow into lasting anchors.

- **Protect what you build.** Use trusts and other estate planning tools to safeguard your assets. If you borrow against land, do so carefully and with a clear plan to repay. Equity is a tool to be used wisely.

- **Teach the next owners.** Walk your heirs through the documents, payments, and the story behind what you have built. Stewardship is complete when understanding is passed along with ownership.

REFLECTION

What does *ownership* mean to me in property, and purpose?

____

____

____

____

____

Who are the *right people* to share my vision with; the ones who can help carry it?

____

____

____

____

____

How am I preparing the next generation to understand the purpose and responsibility of what I am building?

____

____

____

____

____

PRAYER

God,

Thank You for the wisdom to see beyond today and the courage to build for tomorrow. Teach us to steward what we acquire with care, to protect what is entrusted to us, and to pass it on with purpose. Guide our decisions, strengthen our discipline, and help us create legacies that provide stability, dignity, and hope for generations to come. May what we build honor You and bless those who follow.

Amen.

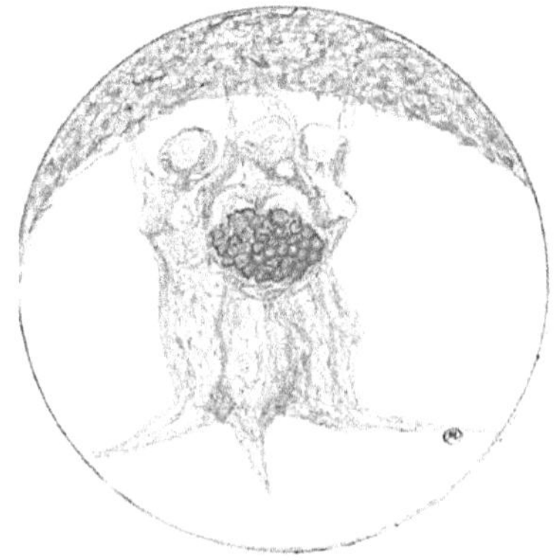

5 – EDUCATE YOURSELF BEYOND THE CLASSROOM

If there was one lesson passed down from my grandmothers to my mother, from my mother to me, and now from me to my daughters, it is this: Never stop learning. Simply stated that if you want to continue to elevate your life, educate your mind. For the women who raised me, education was never confined to a classroom. It wasn't measured by degrees or diplomas. It was measured by curiosity, consistency, and courage. It was about building confidence, cultivating wisdom, and expanding what you thought possible. They understood that knowledge opens doors, sharpens discernment, and protects your future. And because of them, I learned that real education isn't a season of life, it's a lifetime pursuit.

The Scholar with a Grade School Education

For Grandma Mary, who had nothing more than a grammar school education, the irony is profound. She owned the most land out of all my Mothers. While others might have linked education to wealth, her life proved otherwise. Grandma Mary was living proof that wisdom is not limited by formal schooling. She studied life itself, the soil, the seasons, and the human spirit. Her classroom was her community, her lessons written in hard work and faith. And through that learning, she built not only a livelihood but a legacy. Her eighty acres of land became a tangible testament to her belief that knowledge isn't about books, it's about understanding how the world works and how to work within it. She taught me that education and wealth are not always found in the same places and that you can cultivate both if you are willing to learn from every moment, every person, and every experience.

Granny — It's Never Too Late to Learn

Granny taught me that it's never too late to begin again. When I was a little girl, I watched her go back to school to earn her associate's degree from a local community college. She wasn't doing it for recognition or reward, she did it because she believed in growth. She used to say, "When you stop learning, you stop living."

For her, education wasn't about proving herself to anyone, it was about honoring herself: her mind, her potential, and the God who gave her both. Her quiet determination left an imprint on me that outlasted any textbook or lesson plan. She showed me that learning is not an age, a stage, or a status. Learning is an attitude.

Granny also believed in tough love. She understood that some of the most life-shaping lessons are not delivered through comfort, but through correction.

When a niece, nephew, or other family member strayed, she did not turn away. She opened her home, extended love, and helped guide them back onto the right path. As I was growing up, I witnessed many of them show her a special admiration and deep love. What puzzled others never puzzled me, because I always knew she was special.

Her love was firm, yet faithful. It was rooted in the belief that accountability is a form of education, and that guidance given with care can change the course of a life.

Reading as Ritual, Reflection, and Refuge

My mother was the embodiment of lifelong learning. As a licensed clinical social worker, she devoted her career to helping others grow, and even after retirement, she remained a devoted student of the world.

She watched MSNBC, CNN, and every major news network, not for entertainment, but for understanding. She would call me several times a day to share updates, perspectives, and insights on everything from politics to public policy. When my days were too full to keep up with the latest developments, she became my personal newscaster and my favorite teacher, patiently informing me and expanding my understanding of the world. I miss those calls deeply now, those moments of learning that were quietly wrapped in love.

She was also a proud member and later President of the SPLENDOR Book Club, a circle of brilliant women who gathered for more than thirty years to read, debate, and delight in the power of story. She believed reading was not simply entertainment. It was enlightenment. **My SPLENDOR Aunties**, loved my family and surrounded my mom with friendship, laughter, and care. Their presence in her life was a gift, and their love continues to be felt.

I can recall when I was in elementary school, the first credit card my mother applied for was from a bookstore chain called Kroch's & Brentano's. While others opened accounts at department stores, or proudly carried their American Express card, her priority was making sure she could purchase and own books she loved. Through books, my mother explored lives beyond her own, built empathy for people she never met, and strengthened her faith in humanity. She often said, "Education does not stop with graduation. It grows with conversation."

When my daughter Malaika was little, my mother would take her on long visits to bookstores, not quick errands, but unhurried adventures. They spent hours browsing, sitting in quiet corners surrounded by the scent of pages and possibility. They read, explored, and connected. Those trips became a ritual of love and legacy. Today, Malaika reads voraciously, devouring seven-hundred-page novels in days, not because she has to, but because she wants to. Her grandmother made reading sacred, not scholastic. That is how legacy works. It plants seeds that bloom generations later.

Learning Beyond the Walls

True education is not confined to classrooms or credentials. It is found in conversations with elders, in quiet moments of reflection after failure, and in the humility it takes to ask questions you cannot yet answer. It lives in the books you open, the people you listen to, the faith you study, and the risks you take. It is learning from the living.

Shortly after the COVID 19 shutdown, my mother came to live with us so we could create our own safety bubble. We had no idea those months would become the final eighteen months of her life. One night, after she had been with us for a year, my mother shared something that deeply moved me. She told me that every evening my youngest daughter, Nya, would quietly come into the guest room just to talk. I did not realize then that those conversations would become a steady source of wisdom for Nya, lessons she still carries with her today.

Education can give you knowledge, but when it is paired with wisdom and strength, it can empower you in ways you never imagined. What I learned from my Mothers collectively is this… Some of the richest lessons are not taught. They are lived.

Life Application

- **Commit to lifelong learning**. Education does not end with a degree or a classroom. It grows through curiosity, experience, and intention. Read widely, ask thoughtful questions, and seek wisdom from those who have walked the road ahead of you. Study what shapes your life, including your faith, your finances, your culture, and your calling.

- **Feed your mind daily with something that expands your understanding**. Learn from your community by listening to mentors and elders.

- **Approach challenges with curiosity by asking what the moment is teaching you.** Then pass what you learn forward. Share a story, a skill, or a lesson with someone coming behind you. Wisdom becomes legacy when it is lived and shared.

- **Degrees may hang on a wall, but wisdom walks with you.** That is the kind of education no one can take away.

REFLECTION

What subject, skill, or calling is God inviting me to study more deeply right now?

____

____

____

____

____

Whose wisdom do I need to seek or listen to more intentionally in this season?

____

____

____

____

____

What lesson I am learning now should I pass on to strengthen someone else?

____

____

____

____

PRAYER

God,

When I choose to keep learning, I choose to keep growing. As I grow, open my mind to wisdom found in every season, beyond classrooms and credentials. Help me remain curious, humble, and open to the lessons life offers each day. May my learning shape my choices, strengthen my faith, and unlock the future You have designed for me. Guide me to use what I gain to serve others and to leave a legacy rooted in purpose and understanding.

Amen.

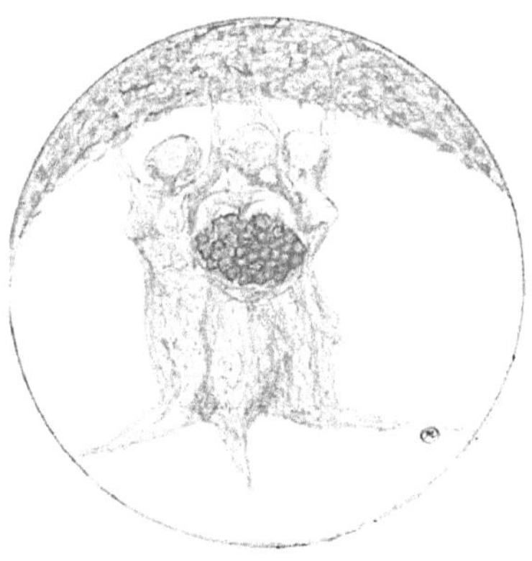

6 – PLAN FOR PEACE BEFORE YOU PASS

One thing that I know for certain as an Estate Planning attorney is that Wills, Trust and proper Estate Planning prevent family division. *Failing to plan causes pain.* Not the kind of pain that fades with time, but the kind that lingers, the kind that fractures families, breeds resentment, and quietly erodes legacies built over generations. The women who raised me understood that love isn't measured only by what you do while you're living, it's reflected in how you prepare for when you're gone. And perhaps no one embodied that truth more clearly than Grandma Mary.

Planning With Purpose

Grandma Mary didn't just acquire 80 acres of land in rural Mississippi, she made certain that land would never divide her family. She had seen what happened to others when property passed without clarity. She had watched neighbors' families fall apart — siblings stop speaking, cousins grow cold, and hard-earned land get swallowed by bitterness and the courthouse.

One particular story stuck with her. She saw a nearby family feud turn ugly after the father died without a will or form of Estate Planning. The property he had worked for his entire life became the very thing that tore his children apart. That sight stayed with her. And in that moment, Grandma Mary made a vow, "My children will not fight over what I worked for."

So, she went to a local attorney in Mississippi, long before "Estate Planning" was a common phrase in our community, and gave him clear instructions to do what was necessary to divide her land upon her death. Each of her children were to inherit their identified portion of the land.

Her modest home sat on a portion of the eight acres, and her youngest daughter was to inherit that piece. Grandma Mary didn't have formal training in law or finance, but she had foresight and faith. Without even realizing it, she was doing what I now spend my professional life teaching and encouraging others to do, estate planning. She planned not because she expected to die soon, but because she wanted to live peacefully knowing her affairs were in order. She didn't wait for probate. She didn't leave it to the family to figure out, or to the probate court to divide and control. She maintained control and planned accordingly.

And in doing so, she preserved more than property, she preserved peace. Her foresight kept our family united, her land protected, and her name honored. Grandma Mary taught us that estate planning isn't just a financial act. Estate Planning is a spiritual one. It's how you turn love into legacy.

Simplicity, Security, and Steadiness

Granny and Papa believed in order and like Grandma Mary, they had a family attorney. As a young child, I recalled going with them to visit their attorney in downtown Chicago. They made certain that they had a Will created even though they only had one child. They knew the importance of planning.. It was their way of making certain that when the time came, there was no confusion nor any uncertainty about what they wanted. Their clarity gave my mother peace. And when my mother later planned her own affairs, she modeled the same calm order they had shown her.

Three generations of women, each with a different level of education, means, and access shared one powerful value: Don't leave chaos as your legacy.

Order That Brings Peace

When my Mom passed away, her affairs were impeccable. There was no scrambling, no searching, and no second-guessing. Everything had been organized and thought through, not only because she was meticulous, but because she was merciful. She knew the importance of order. She had witnessed other family members go through utter chaos when a loved one passed away. She made certain I had access to every account, password, etc. so that I could easily manage her affairs. When she passed, there was no uncertainty or confusion. My mother lived with intention and she passed with peace knowing that everything was in order.

Breaking the Silence Around Planning

That kind of intentionality is rare. But it shouldn't be. Too often in the African American community, we avoid conversations about Estate Planning and other end-of-life decisions.

We treat them as taboo, as if discussing death will somehow invite it. We promise ourselves we'll "get to it later," not realizing that later is never guaranteed.

As an estate planning attorney, I've seen it too many times, families unraveling in the fog of grief, lost between emotion and confusion, unsure of who's in charge or what their loved one truly wanted. Grief and chaos don't mix well. And no family deserves to mourn while trying to solve a legal puzzle. That's why I tell every client, and every friend, the same truth my Mothers lived out loud.

Estate Planning is essential to prevent family division. Whether it is drafting a will, naming a power of attorney, or creating a trust, these decisions matter. They speak when you cannot. They protect what you have built and ensure that your children, grandchildren, and even your community can benefit from your life rather than be burdened by your loss.

My Mothers taught me, and I now teach others, that love requires preparation. If you love your family, put your plans in writing. Do not leave clarity to chance or assume others will figure it out. Give them the gift of direction, certainty, and peace. A will or a Trust is more than a legal document, it is your final love letter.

Estate planning documents are more than paperwork. They are your legacy, preserved.

Life Application

- **Honor your love through preparation.** Grandma Mary taught me to think beyond today and build toward the future. Granny showed me that clear plans bring peace to the family. Mom reminded me that the strongest love is intentional and expressed through action.

- **Take time to put your wishes in writing.** Create an estate plan that provides clear direction for your assets. Prepare a will, choose trusted decision makers, and consider tools such as trusts to protect what you have built. Offer clarity, guidance, and comfort..

- **Support a loved one in creating a proper plan**. Encourage them to work with a professional who can ensure their wishes are accurately protected through carefully drafted estate planning documents. Sometimes people need the support and direction that you are able to provide. **Estate planning is not about fear.** It is an act of love, stewardship, and intention that secures the legacy you worked so hard to create.

REFLECTION

What do I need or someone close to me need to do in order to ensure that there is a plan in writing?

____

____

____

____

What do I want in place so what I have built or acquired continues to serve those I love?

____

____

____

____

If I write a plan to ease the burden on my loved ones, what would it be?

____

____

____

____

PRAYER

Lord,

Grant me the clarity and courage to plan with wisdom and love. Quiet my fears and guide my thoughts so that my decisions reflect care, stewardship, and responsibility. Help me to prepare not out of worry, but out of peace, knowing that thoughtful planning can be an act of love. May what I put in place today bring comfort, stability, and assurance to those I cherish tomorrow. Lead me as I plan, and let peace be the outcome of every step I take.

Amen

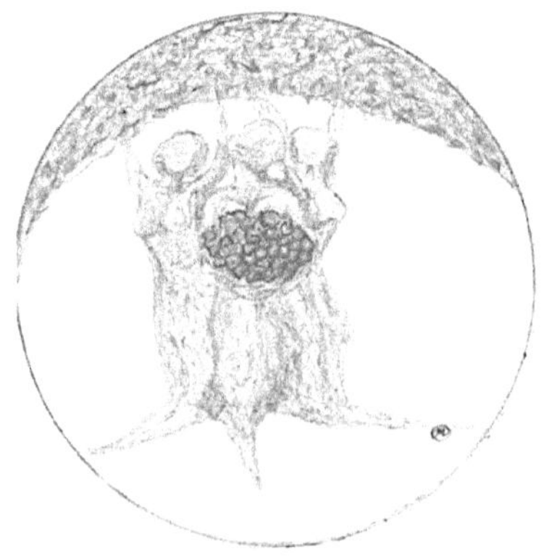

TIMELESS
22 LESSONS OF FAITH, HOPE & LOVE

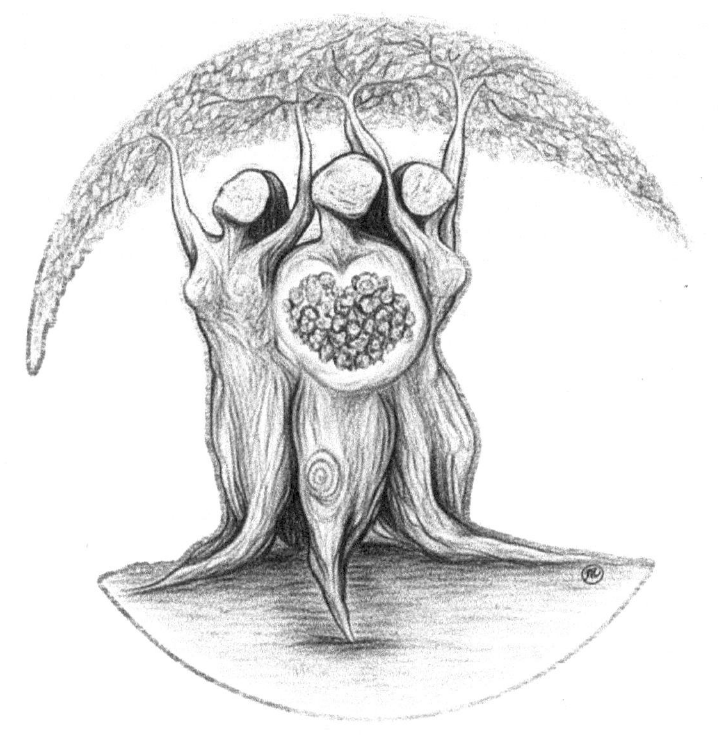

*"Estate planning documents
are more than paperwork.
They are your legacy, preserved."*
- Deadra Woods Stokes

LOVE, FAMILY AND RELATIONSHIPS

TIMELESS

22 LESSONS OF FAITH, HOPE & LOVE

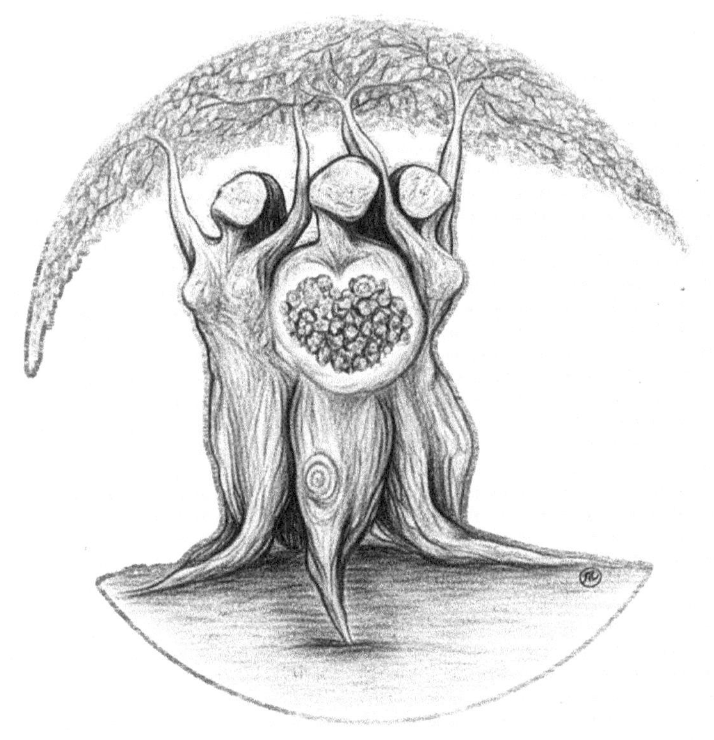

"*Choose a mate who builds with you —
not just boasts beside you.*"

- Barbara J. Woods

7 – MARRY VISION, NOT JUST CHARM

One of the most powerful lessons I learned from the women who raised me is this: the person you choose to walk through life with will either anchor your purpose or interrupt your peace. They never said it quite that way, but they lived it. Through their choices, sacrifices, and steadfast faith, my Mothers showed me that while charm may attract attention, vision sustains connection.

When it comes to marriage and partnership, you need more than someone who looks good on paper or turns heads in a room. You need someone who shares your values, sees your potential, and is willing to build a life with you, not simply shine beside you.

The Blueprint of Partnership

Both of my grandmothers married young and remained married through much of their adult lives. They were devoted wives, yes, but they were also strategic women who understood that love alone would not sustain a family.

They respected their husbands, yet they recognized a deeper truth. Emotional commitment means little without economic stability. To protect their children's future, they knew the family's name had to be tied to real estate and ownership, not merely survival.

Grandma Mary and Granny worked alongside their husbands with vision that reached far beyond the present day. They stretched every dollar, safeguarded every deed, and labored quietly but intentionally to build something lasting. They loved deeply, but they led decisively. They never confused submission with silence.

Their marriages were grounded in shared purpose, prayer, and perseverance, not empty promises or performative affection. They built wealth through wisdom, doing so in an era when women were rarely expected to speak about money, let alone manage it.

A Modern Shift — The Evolution of Ownership

For much of my childhood, my parents lived in elite high-rises in Hyde Park, where comfort and convenience took precedence over ownership. It was a beautiful lifestyle, but it was not grounded in the kind of generational wealth my grandmothers had built in Mississippi and on the South Side of Chicago. It was not until I was in college that my parents began investing in real estate, and not until I was in law school that my mother purchased her first piece of property after her divorce from my father.

By that time, she was determined to own something tangible that would outlast both her career and her marriage. She often reflected that if she had prioritized ownership earlier, she could have built even greater wealth to pass along. Even so, her story, like those of my grandmothers, stands as a testament to the power of independence and the wisdom of vision. My mother's later-in-life real estate purchase symbolized more than financial freedom. It represented emotional liberation and the decision to plant her own flag and define her worth not by relationship, but by resolve.

Discernment and Dignity

Mom modeled what it meant to love wisely and live freely. Later in life, she recognized that same balance in the man I married. She knew Paul long before I did. She knew his family, his heart, and the values that shaped him. By the time we became partners, she did not have to wonder who he was. She already knew.

She loved him deeply and respected him immensely. She saw how he treated me, not as an accessory, but as an equal. She noticed his calm presence, his discipline, and unwavering faith. Mom once said, "If I had a son, I would want him to be just like Paul." That was her highest compliment, and she meant every word.

Paul has never been threatened by my drive or unsettled by my success. He has never asked me to shrink to make room for his ego. Instead, he has stood beside me as a steady partner, not in competition, but in true partnership. He makes me laugh when the days grow heavy. He prays with me when decisions become difficult. He builds with me, brick by brick, dream by dream, day by day.

He does not merely occupy space in my life. He adds to it. Together, we are building a legacy that reflects everything my Mothers taught me. Love without partnership is fragile, but love built on purpose endures. Mom often said, "The right partner does not compete with your calling. They complement it."

Personal Reflection

There was a time, like many others, when I was drawn to charm, to charisma without character and chemistry without commitment. But the women who raised me taught me that what lasts is not always loud or glittering. What lasts is vision. It is character. It is shared faith. That is what I found in Paul.

Although my grandmothers passed before meeting him, I know they would have embraced him fully. He reflects the principles they lived by: humility, discipline, devotion, and God-first leadership. He loves with strength and gentleness. He listens with his heart. He has never made me question whether I am fully seen, heard, or valued.

So here is what I pass on to you. Do not be swept away by the surface. Be anchored in substance. Do not marry potential. Marry purpose. Choose a partner who aligns with your vision and shares your values. Legacy requires more than love. It requires labor, loyalty, and long-term faith.

When storms come, and they will, you do not need someone who only shines in the sunshine. You need someone who will pick up the tools, whisper a prayer, and help rebuild when the rain falls. Charm fades. Appearances change. Vision, however, is what builds something that lasts.

Life Application

- **The right relationship does more than feel good.** It builds something meaningful, lasting, and worthy of being passed down. True love is not measured by fleeting emotion, but by what you create together over time.

- **Choose character over charm and purpose over potential**. Alignment matters. Shared values and spiritual agreement ground a partnership when life becomes difficult. Legacy requires teamwork. The right partner pours into you, supports your dreams, and commits to building alongside you.

- **Storms will come**. Choose someone who stays, prays, and works through the hard seasons rather than walking away when the work gets heavy. Vision sustains love. What you build together will always outlast the butterflies you began with.

REFLECTION

Does this person make me better? Do they inspire growth in faith, discipline, and purpose?

____

____

____

____

____

Are we building something that matters?- Is there direction, not just affection?

____

____

____

____

Can we weather storms together? Are we both willing to repair what life tries to tear down?

____

____

____

____

PRAYER

God,

Help me choose partnership with vision, wisdom, and purpose — not pressure or fantasy.

Amen.

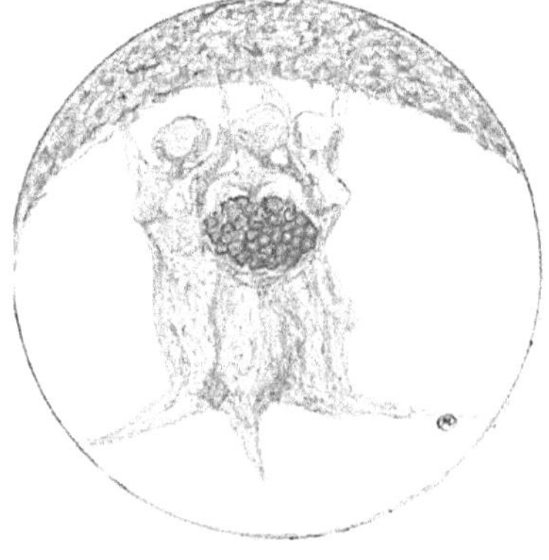

8 – TOUGH LOVE IS STILL LOVE

When I think about the way my Mothers raised their children, I realize that discipline was never about punishment; it was a way of protection. They loved us enough to correct us, guide us, and shape our character, even when it wasn't easy or appreciated. They understood a truth that has stayed with me all my life: "Love that never corrects eventually neglects."

Correction was their way of saying, "I see your potential and I refuse to let you settle for less." Their discipline wasn't a withdrawal of love, it was proof of it.

Growing up, I never doubted that I was loved. I knew there were certain things I couldn't get away with. Not because the women who raised me were harsh or unforgiving, but because they loved me enough to correct me. Their expectations were high and standards clear. They wanted and expected me to be excellent. They understood something the world often forgets: Discipline is a form of love.

The Firm Hand of Wisdom

Granny was known in our family for her unapologetic brand of "tough love." She didn't sugarcoat truth or dance around feelings. If you were wrong, she told you directly, calmly, and with absolute clarity. Relatives would often send their children to her when they needed structure. A few weeks in her home could transform a rebellious spirit into a respectful one.

She didn't need to raise her voice. Her look said enough. Her tone carried weight and she demanded respect because she gave it. She expected accountability because she practiced it herself. Somehow, no matter how firm her correction, we always knew it came from love. You left her presence a little straighter, wiser, and a lot more grateful.

Quiet Authority, Lasting Impact

Grandma Mary had a gentler touch, but her influence ran deep. Her lessons weren't always spoken, they were modeled. She corrected through consistency and quiet strength. If she gave you advice, you listened. If she gave you a look, you knew exactly what that meant. Her discipline wasn't loud, but it was clear. And it always came wrapped in love. She showed me that correction doesn't have to be cruel to be effective. Sometimes the calmest voice carries the clearest truth.

Grace With a Backbone

Then there was Mom. She was the perfect balance of grace and grit. She gave me room to express myself, but never enough to lose my way. She was protective and present, the mom who picked up me and my friends from parties in the middle of the night, driving miles to drop everyone home safely. And if she thought I made poor decisions, she didn't explode, she simply explained.

She told me and my friends the truth, even when we didn't want to hear it. That's how I learned that love isn't just comfort. Love is correction. My Mothers didn't correct to control. They corrected to protect."

The Love That Shapes, Not Shames

Through their example, I learned that love is not always soft, it's also strong, it sets boundaries, and it demands better. It holds you accountable, not to shame you, but to shape you. It doesn't ignore mistakes; it teaches through them. In a world that often mistakes correction for criticism, my Mothers taught me that silence is not kindness. You don't watch people you love walk toward destruction and say nothing. They showed me that truth, spoken in love, is one of the purest expressions of care.

The Gift of Tough Love

Because of their firm but faithful guidance, I learned discipline. I learned responsibility and how to admit when I was wrong. I correct my course, and keep striving for more. At the time, I didn't always like it but looking back, I'm eternally grateful. Their tough love didn't just keep me in line; it kept me whole. It protected me from choices that could have cost me my future. It built resilience where rebellion might have taken root.

Legacy Lesson

So here's what I now pass to you: Correction is not the absence of love, it's the evidence of it. We need people in our lives who love us enough to tell us the truth gently when they can, firmly when they must. And we need to be that kind of person for others. Love that only comforts will never change you. Love that corrects? That's the kind that grows you. Tough love saved me more than once. Tough love saved those blessed to have my Mothers in their lives. "Tough love" was one of the purest, most protective forms of love I ever received.

Life Application

- **Correction is care.** Love that corrects is a love that protects.

- **Boundaries build character.** Clear expectations guide growth and maturity.

- **Silence is not kindness.** Truth spoken in love prevents greater harm.

- **Strength and grace belong together.** Firm correction can still be compassionate.

- **Discipline shapes destiny.** Guidance today safeguards tomorrow.

REFLECTION

How do I respond to correction on constructive criticism? Do I receive it as love or react as if it's an attack?

____

____

____

____

____

Where do I need to set loving boundaries? Protection requires structure.

____

____

____

____

____

Who in my life needs truth spoken in love?

____

____

____

____

PRAYER

Lord,

Help me give and receive correction with grace,
knowing it is rooted in love and designed for my good.

Amen.

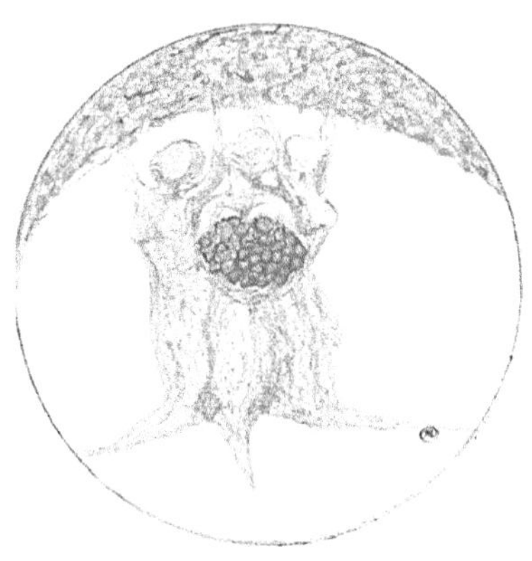

9 – GIVE BACK WITHOUT LOSING YOURSELF

When I reflect on this lesson from my Mothers, I can almost hear them collectively reminding me: "You can't give from an empty well." My mother said those words often, sometimes gently, sometimes urgently, always with love. It was her way of telling me to slow down, to breathe, to remember that I am human before I am anyone else's help.

From my mother and grandmothers, I learned one of the most sacred truths: You can pour into others, but you must also pour into yourself. Loving people. Serving family. Supporting your community. Pouring into your calling. All of that matters deeply but never at the cost of your health, your peace, or your joy. The women who raised me modeled service as a calling and self-respect as a requirement.

Giving With Boundaries, Serving With Wisdom

Mom lived this balance with grace. She was the ultimate giver. To many, she was a mentor, a caretaker to my grandfather, a confidante, and a trusted friend. She gave freely, lovingly, and often. Yet even as she poured into everyone around her, she never stopped doing the things she loved that nourished her spirit and her soul.

For more than thirty years, she remained devoted to her monthly book club. Reading was her greatest passion, and it continually fed her inner life. She also loved church and the friendships and relationships that were formed in that sacred space. Attending church every Sunday brought her joy, and singing in the choir was what she loved most of all. Cooking was another expression of her love, especially when it came to her favorite holiday, Thanksgiving. She delighted in the preparation, in the care poured into each dish, and in the joy she felt watching those she loved enjoy the food she prepared.

She encouraged me to make time for the things I loved to do. She emphasized the importance of creating space for what brings peace and restoration. She understood what many women forget, that the more roles we carry, the more intentional we must be about refilling ourselves. She knew how easily women, especially mothers, leaders, and caregivers, can lose themselves while caring for everyone else, and she consistently reminded me not to let that happen.

Check-Ins That Became Lifelines

What I miss most are my mother's calls. Those simple, steady, everyday conversations that carried far more meaning than the words themselves. Where are you? What are you doing? Did you make it to the gym? How was your day?

At the time, I did not always recognize it, but those calls were care disguised as conversation. They were her way of saying, take care of yourself, because you matter too. They were not about control. They were about connection. They were her gentle way of making sure I was giving something back to myself while I was out in the world giving to everyone else.

More Than Physical — A Call to Wholeness

Her reminders weren't only about the body, they are also about the soul. She taught me that self-care isn't just massages or vacations. It's boundaries, rest without guilt, laughter in the middle of chaos. It's silence when the world gets too loud. It's knowing that you are worthy of nurture and peace, even when no one else stops to ask how you are doing.

That's the part of her voice I still hear in my spirit, the gentle nudge to pause, breathe, stretch, and preserve the woman I am. Not just for those who need me, but for the woman I am still becoming.

Peace in the Garden

Grandma Mary found solitude in tending to her farm while producing for her family and the community. She sought peace in cultivating her farm.

Grandma Mary found self-preservation in tending her land. Her farm wasn't just labor, it was refuge. Working in her farm was quiet time among the rows of vegetables that she grew. Those rows gave her peace, strength, and time with God. In caring for the earth, she cared for herself. She taught me that sometimes tending to others begins with tending to your own garden, literally and spiritually. Today I enjoy my time in my seasonal garden just like my Grandma Mary.

The Legacy of Self-Preservation

My Mothers served. They gave. They led. But they never disappeared. They understood that neglecting yourself is not humility, it is erosion. They taught me that you cannot build a lasting legacy if you are crumbling quietly beneath it.

So I remind myself and every person I mentor: Help your neighbor. Raise your children. Serve your church.

Lead your team. But don't forget yourself. Water your soul. Feed your joy. Rest your body. Because nothing grows where neglect lives. Even the strongest person needs time to restore so they can continue to rise.

Life Application

- **Self-neglect is not humility.** Caring for others begins with caring for yourself. Service should not require the loss of your health, peace, or identity.

- **Boundaries are protection, not selfishness.** Boundaries preserve the strength God has entrusted to you and allow you to serve with wisdom rather than exhaustion.

- **Give from abundance, not depletion.** Keep your well full to overflow. Wholeness is your greatest gift. A restored you blesses everyone around you.

- **Tend to your own garden.** Nourish your body, mind, and spirit so that your growth is sustainable and your service enduring.

REFLECTION

How do I care for myself intentionally?

____

____

____

____

____

Where am I giving more than I have? How do I make adjustments to honor my peace?

____

____

____

____

____

Who pours back into me?

____

____

____

____

PRAYER

God,

Help me give from overflow, not emptiness. Teach me to honor the person I am, not just the roles I serve.

Amen.

.

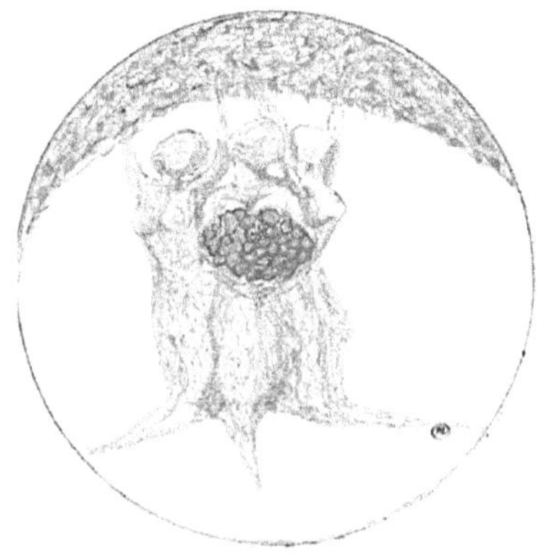

10 – RAISE LEGACY BEARERS

My Mothers collectively imparted a truth that continues to guide how I understand parenting and mentorship: we do not raise children merely to survive the world, we raise them to shape it. Children are not meant to be managed. They are meant to be formed. Their responsibility was never limited to keeping us safe in the moment, but to preparing us for the future we would one day lead.

Through their example, I learned that our calling is to instill identity, so children know who they are and whose they are; to instill purpose, so they understand that their lives carry meaning and mission; and to instill preparation, so they can walk confidently into rooms designed to challenge them and still rise.

My Mothers raised their children and grandchildren with vision. They recognized leadership in small beginnings and nurtured behavior and belief. Obedience was never the final goal. Becoming was.

Raising children is a sacred assignment. For Grandma Mary, Granny, and Mom, it was never simply about survival or good manners. It was about legacy. They believed children should be loved and protected, but also equipped with history, purpose, faith, courage, and confidence. They prepared us to carry something greater than our own names, to walk forward bearing the prayers, principles, and sacrifices of the generations before us.

They were not just raising children. They were raising future leaders, homeowners, college graduates, business owners, and community builders.

Every Action Was an Investment

Nothing they did was accidental. Every story shared around the dinner table, every correction offered in love, every dollar saved, and every prayer whispered over our heads was a deliberate deposit into our future. They did not simply want us to make it. They wanted us to build upon it. They were architects of continuity, women who thought beyond the moment, beyond themselves, and beyond their time. They understood that legacy does not happen by chance. It happens by choice.

Continuing the Blueprint

I've carried that same principle into how I've raised my daughters. From the beginning, I wanted them to know not just who they were, but more importantly, "whose" they were. I wanted them to walk into rooms with their heads held high, knowing the shoulders they stood on. I wanted them to understand that success isn't about possessions, it's about purpose. That the true measure of achievement is not what you collect, but what you contribute. They were raised to know that their lineage is not one of luck; it's one of labor, prayer, and divine preparation.

The Reinforcement of a Matriarch

My Mother played a pivotal role in helping me raise them that way. She didn't just pour into me, she poured in my daughters. She read to them, prayed with them, and challenged them. She modeled quiet dignity and unwavering discipline. Mom showed them that legacy isn't just property or wealth, legacy is *preparation*. It's the ability to live with intention and to pass on wisdom that multiplies across generations. She reminded them, as she reminded me, that we are all links in a sacred chain and that our strength lies in what we choose to carry forward.

The Lesson I Tell My Daughters

Even now, I tell my girls, "You are not here just to exist. You are here to build, to heal, and to lead. You are here to carry forward the vision your grandmothers saw when they bought land, built homes, and refused to settle for less than God's best. You are your ancestors' greatest dream come true. You are walking on ground they prayed over. You are living the dreams they dared to see. And one day, someone will stand on your shoulders, so stand tall."

I have come to understand that legacy is not a single moment you leave behind. Legacy is a mindset you choose and live out every day. One of my daughter Malaika's favorite reminders captures that truth perfectly: *"Fortify your mind."* My youngest daughter, Nya, who is a finance major, has especially embraced Great Grandmother Mary's wisdom when it comes to managing money. Even at a young age, she stays focused on her credit score and is intentional with every dollar she earns through scholarships and small jobs. She budgets with the same discipline Granny lived by, while setting goals and working toward financial milestones with confidence and purpose.

When I look at my daughters, I see my grandmothers in them. I tell them often that their strength, their values, and their drive come from a foundation that was built long before them. I remind them to keep striving, to stay grounded, and to be their very best, because the groundwork has already been laid.

Legacy Lesson

Children grow quickly, but legacies are built slowly through patience, intention, and faith. It is not enough to raise children who are simply polite or successful. We must help raise legacy bearers who understand who they are, what they have inherited, and what they are called to protect and pass forward. This lesson is not limited to mothers with biological children. It can be passed down by an aunt, an uncle, a friend, or any mother figure, and it applies to anyone who has been called to mentor another person.

Yes, it is part of your purpose to nurture their dreams, encourage their gifts, and celebrate their victories. Yet it is equally important to teach them history, to teach them ownership, and to show them how to manage money, how to pray, how to lead with integrity, and how to choose partners with purpose. One day, they will pass those lessons on to someone else.

When that day comes, they will remember that legacy was not simply something they received. It was something they were entrusted to continue. In the end, we are all called to help raise legacy bearers, and the future depends on how faithfully we prepare them.

Life Application

- **Raise legacy bearers.** Protect and prepare your children. Equip them with wisdom, tools, and confidence to shape the future, and survive it.

- **Ground them in identity.** Identity is the foundation of legacy. Instill pride in who they are and whose they are so they never shrink in spaces meant for their growth and greatness.

- **Teach purpose early.** Help them understand that their lives carry assignment, mission, and divine intention. Purpose gives direction to their gifts and meaning to their work.

- **Prepare them intentionally.** Preparation turns dreams into destiny. Reading, teaching, boundaries, discipline, and exposure become building blocks of a life well lived and a legacy sustained.

- **Parent with generational vision.** Legacy is not accidental; it is cultivated through intentional choices: conversations, corrections, celebrations, and prayers are investments that shape future harvests.

REFLECTION

What am I teaching the children and young people in my life?

____

____

____

____

____

Am I preparing those I am called to mentor for leadership or just for survival?

____

____

____

____

What am I shaping for the next generation? How will I know they can carry it with courage and conviction?

____

____

____

____

PRAYER

God,

When I raise children with pride in their lineage, when I equip them with the tools to lead, when I nurture their calling with prayer and preparation, I'm not just raising children, I am raising legacy bearers and the future is depending on me to do it well.

Amen.

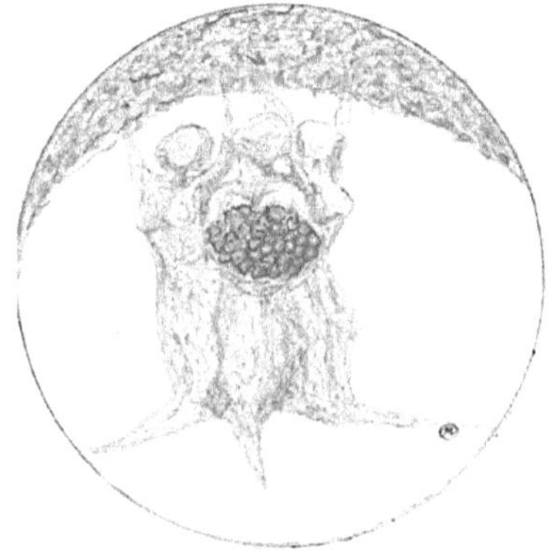

11 – THE WISDOM OF DISCERNMENT

Discernment in relationships is one of the greatest gifts my Mothers ever gave me. They taught me early that who you walk with shapes where you end up and how well you get there. My mother would often remind me, "Some people are meant to teach you, not travel with you." That was her gentle way of saying that not everyone who enters your life is meant to stay.

Not every cheer is sincere. Not every open door is divine. She wanted me to learn how to recognize the difference.

From Transaction to Transformation

When I was younger, I believed networking was about exchange. I often asked myself what a person could do for me or how a connection might advance my goals. As I grew, however, I began to understand the deeper truth my Mothers lived by. The best relationships are not transactional. They are transformational.

Meaningful people stretch you. They challenge you. They help you become more than you imagined possible. True connection enriches your character more than it fills your calendar.

The Wisdom of Discernment

Granny delivered life lessons wrapped in metaphor. She often said, "You cannot water every plant in the garden. Some are not meant to grow in your soil." At the time, I thought she was teaching me about gardening; she was teaching me about boundaries. Granny understood that time is like water. It is precious, limited, and necessary. When you pour into the wrong people, you end up depleted rather than developed. Granny encouraged me to surround myself with people who bring sunlight, not shadows.

Community Over Crowds

Grandma Mary Nealy Little was intentional about the company she kept. She didn't need crowds, she cultivated **community**. Women gathered with her to quilt, to pray, to share stories. They built more than blankets, they built belonging. Her relationships were rooted in faith, fellowship, and shared strength. She taught me that popularity fades but partnership endures.

Graceful Release

My mother loved wholeheartedly and wisely. Her kindness was powerful but never careless. She would often tell me, "Deadra, everyone is not meant to go with you into every season." She knew how to love without clinging, forgive without opening old doors, and bless people from a distance when necessary. She taught me that letting go can be an act of love, that boundaries are blessings, and that discernment protects your destiny. Her example freed me from guilt and gave me permission to choose peace over proximity.

The Art of Selective Energy

Through motherhood, leadership, and ministry, I learned what my Mothers always knew: Discernment isn't about judgment but stewardship. Every moment is a seed, every relationship is soil. Choose wisely where you plant, not everything you water will grow you.

Prosperity is more than success; it is peace, clarity, emotional and spiritual wealth. The right people water you. The company you keep becomes the life you live. Legacy grows best in the gardens of genuine connection. I see the pattern clearly: My Mothers taught me how to invest where love expands, not where energy evaporates. They wanted me to flourish, not fracture. Mom always said: "Grow where you are celebrated, not where you are tolerated." In tolerated spaces, you shrink. In celebrated spaces, you soar. Protect your spirit, your space, and your peace; your destiny depends on it.

Life Application

- **Honor discernment as sacred.** Protect your time and energy as valuable resources entrusted to you.

- **Choose growth-focused relationships.** Surround yourself with people who challenge you, stretch you, and uplift your purpose.

- **Respect boundaries as wisdom.** Letting go is not weakness. It is often the clearest expression of maturity and self-respect.

- **Value community over crowds.** Quality connections endure longer than convenience or popularity.

- **Be intentional about where you plant your energy.** Bloom where you are nourished, and prune where growth is no longer possible.

REFLECTION

What relationships give you strength and which ones that drain it?

____

____

____

____

____

Am I planting seeds or losing soil? (Identify where you're overwatering without growth.)

____

____

____

____

____

Do my relationships align with my calling? (Surround yourself with people who support your purpose.)

____

____

____

____

____

PRAYER

Lord,

Reveal the relationships that are watering my purpose and give me peace to release what no longer aligns with where You are taking me.

Amen.

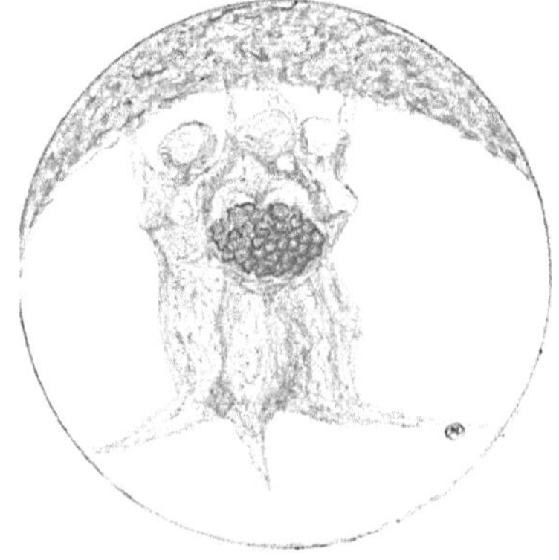

12 – HOW THEY TREAT THEIR MOTHER IS KEY TO HOW THEY WILL TREAT YOU

Someone once told me that the two hardest jobs in the world require no formal training, being a spouse and being a parent. My mother agreed, but through her work as a social worker, she added an important layer of grace. She would often say, "Some people do not know how to parent because they never had good examples." Because of that, she believed we must extend compassion, especially to parents.

Biblical wisdom: "Honor thy father and thy mother." Exodus 20:12 (KJV) Honoring does not mean pretending parents were perfect. It means recognizing their humanity. Respect does not excuse abuse; my mother was clear that in harmful relationships, love and respect may need to be practiced from a distance. She was also firm about this truth. "Watch how people treat their Mothers. That is how they will treat you one day," Mom would say. Disrespect is a habit, and habits travel.

A Mother's Measuring Stick

At first, I assumed her warning applied only to dating. But as I matured, I realized it applies in every relationship: Friendships. Partnerships. Leadership.

Community. How someone treats the woman who carried them, nurtured them, or sacrificed for them reveals their capacity for gratitude and humility.

Character isn't found in titles or charm. It shows up in tone. In patience. In how we handle those who owe us nothing and have given us everything.

Life has shown me the truth of my Mothers' wisdom. I have seen polished and successful people speak to their Mothers with sharp tongues and cold hearts, and that same cruelty later surfaced in their marriages and friendships. I have also seen people raised through hardship choose forgiveness, tenderness, and honor, proving that maturity is a decision, not a circumstance.

It is easy to love when love is easy. It is divine to love through imperfections. Respect for one's mother reflects respect for humanity.

The Blueprint of Respect

Each of the women who raised me modeled her own expression of honoring others. Mom showed love proven daily. She believed integrity reveals itself first in private, in how you speak to those who know your weaknesses and love you anyway.

Granny modeled respect through accountability. She was a mother to one, but a role model to many. She corrected behavior without shaming the heart and often reminded children, "You do not owe me, but you ought to respect me." Discipline, for her, was a ministry of love.

Grandma Mary embodied dignity that commanded honor. She never demanded reverence. Her life earned it. Watching how others treated her taught me who truly understood respect and who merely performed it. People reveal themselves in how they honor the elderly, how they handle disagreement, and how they treat those who can offer nothing in return.

The Mirror of Character

Character is not revealed in a single moment. It is revealed through patterns. Now, when new people enter my life, I pay attention and I ask myself a few questions: Do they speak of their mother with compassion or contempt? Do they show honor when she is present and grace when she is absent? Do they acknowledge her sacrifices and humanity?

The way a person treats their mother often becomes the blueprint for how they handle love, conflict, commitment, and ultimately, how they will treat you.

Life Application

- **Honor begins at home.** Character rises or falls in how we treat the ones who raised us, not because they were perfect, but because we choose to honor the love that brought us here. The way someone treats their mother often reflects how they will treat others. Grace is essential because parents are imperfect people who gave what they had, and they deserve to be met with empathy.

- **Private behavior matters most.** Tone, patience, and compassion reveal a person's true character long before public appearances do. Patterns do not lie.

- **Disrespect repeated over time leads to destruction later, so believe what consistent behavior shows you.** Maturity chooses kindness, and forgiveness and gratitude are signs of spiritual strength and emotional growth.

REFLECTION

How do I honor those who gave me life, whether biological, adoptive, or chosen?

____

____

____

____

____

How can I show grace, even when history is painful?

____

____

____

____

What patterns of honor or dishonor am I modeling for the next generation?

____

____

____

____

PRAYER

Lord,

Give me a spirit of honor, to love with grace, to forgive with wisdom, and to reflect Your character in every relationship, especially with those who nurtured my beginning.

Amen.

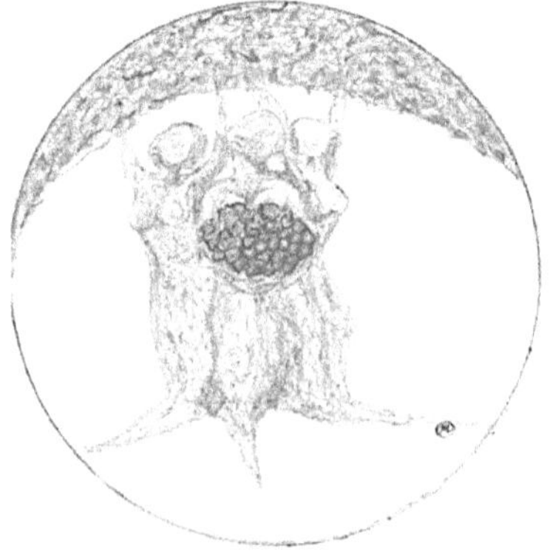

13 – WHAT THEY SHARE ABOUT OTHERS, THEY WILL SHARE ABOUT YOU

Choose your friends wisely and those you choose to confide in, choose even wiser! My mother and grandmothers were truth tellers. They didn't sugarcoat much, and when this lesson came, it usually arrived with a side glance and a knowing look. That one line, "If they talk about everybody, they're talking about you too," was a warning and a prophecy. And over time, I learned just how right they were.

The Trap of Gossip

Gossip is a subtle thief. It does not break in with noise. It seeps in quietly, disguised as conversation. It feels harmless at first, framed as just sharing or just venting, but before you realize it, it steals something sacred, your peace, your focus, and your spiritual clarity.

My mother would always say, *"Be careful where you sit and what you listen to, because spirits travel through conversation."* I did not fully understand that as a child, but now I know exactly what she meant. Negativity is contagious. Words carry energy. When you listen long enough, you begin to absorb the tone, the doubt, and the bitterness that do not even belong to you. When gossip fills your ears, it slowly dulls your discernment, and you stop hearing God's whispers because your attention is consumed by noise.

The Wisdom of My Mothers

Granny was a woman of clarity and courage. She had no tolerance for foolishness. Her rule was simple: *"If you don't have the courage to say it to their face, keep it off your tongue."* She believed that integrity wasn't just about what you did, it was about what you said when the person wasn't in the room.

Grandma Mary, on the other hand, embodied quiet wisdom. She didn't argue or correct. I'm certain, based on her quiet wisdom, she was never a woman who had time nor tolerated gossip of any kind. My grandmothers were from an era where children never sat in the room nor participated during adult conversation. if I was given an opportunity to sit amongst the grown folk, I'm more than certain Grandma Mary would excuse herself from the chaotic negative discussion.

The Discipline of Discernment

Through the years, I've learned to apply this wisdom in every setting, personal, professional, and spiritual. Not all conversations are worthy of your presence. Not every circle is sacred. Energy is precious. Protect it. You don't have to announce your exit, roll your eyes, or lecture anyone. Just gracefully remove yourself from the noise. Stillness is strength. Distance is discernment. Peace is power. Sometimes, peace is found in walking away and not proving a point.

Life Application

- **How someone talks about others is a preview of how they will talk about you.** Gossip does not have favorites. It has targets, and everyone eventually becomes one. The company you keep shapes your spirit; choose people who speak life, practice honor, celebrate others, and build rather than destroy.

- **Conversation reveals character.** The mouth reflects the heart, and what is spoken eventually tells the truth.

- **Gossip steals peace.** Where negativity is constant, joy cannot thrive. Patterns do not lie. Pay attention. If someone regularly talks about others, they will talk about you. Words carry spirit, and what you listen to slowly influences who you become.

- **Discernment is a shield.** Not every voice deserves access to your ears or your energy. Sometimes walking away is an act of wisdom, not avoidance. Silence and distance can be powerful boundaries. Peace is not a luxury. It is a necessity. Protect it carefully, because your purpose depends on it.

REFLECTION

What conversations drain my spirit? Is it time to stand up and walk away?

____

____

____

____

____

Do my words reflect who I truly am? Am I building up or tearing down?

____

____

____

____

How can I model integrity in every discussion?

____

____

____

____

PRAYER

Lord,

Help me guard my ears, my words, and spirit. Make me a vessel of peace, truth, and wisdom always.

Amen.

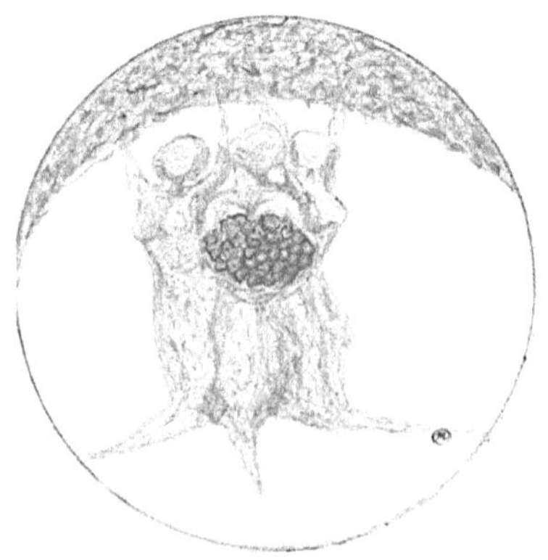

WISDOM, WORK, & INNER STRENGTH

14 – RESILIENCE NEEDS NO APOLOGY

Your strength is your inheritance and it is your gift to the world. Yet as Black women, we are often met with whispers that try to shrink our shine. You hear it in the corners of rooms, in the quiet grumbles just loud enough to wound: *"She is too much!"* And somehow, the sting deepens when the voice sounds familiar, when the person casting the doubt looks like you, knows your story, or shares your struggle. My Mothers taught me and now I pass this on to you: You're not too much. You are exactly enough for the purpose God placed inside you.

One of the most subtle and dangerous messages society sends, especially to women, and particularly to Black women, is this: *Tone it down. Shrink a little. Fit the box.* But purpose refuses confinement. And calling cannot be contained. Too confident. Too vocal. Too ambitious. Too accomplished. Too strong.

And slowly, even the most powerful among us begin to shrink. We tuck away our brilliance. We downplay our success. We apologize for our presence. Not because we're ashamed, but because we've been conditioned to make others comfortable.

The Cost of Shrinking

I know that struggle intimately. I've led classrooms, owned businesses and served in leadership roles in organizations. I have taught, built, served, and raised. Yet there were moments when I'd hear myself saying things like, "*Oh, it's nothing*," or "*I'm just doing my part*, "as though excellence needed an apology.

In truth, I was doing the work of five people with grace, faith, and grit. But somewhere along the way, humility got confused with hiding. And then I'd hear my mother's or grandmother's voice in my head, reminding me who I am.

The Loud Pride of Love

Granny would never let me forget my worth. She passed in 1983, my senior year of high school, but her voice still echoes in my heart. She was my biggest cheerleader, the woman who bragged about me to anyone who'd listen. Neighbors, church members, strangers at the store, it never really mattered. It wasn't vanity. It was validation. If it mattered to me, it mattered to her. And she made sure the world knew it.

At times, I'd blush or whisper, "Granny, please stop telling everybody." Looking back, I understand she was proud of me and saw me as the manifestation of her prayers. Her boasting wasn't arrogance. It was testimony. From her, I learned this truth: strength is not something to hide, you honor. it There is nothing wrong with walking boldly in your calling. Confidence becomes offensive only when it's used to elevate self while diminishing others. But when you walk in your purpose with humility and clarity, your strength becomes a light. A light that liberates and inspires everyone around you.

I honor that lineage of strength: The quiet strength of Grandma Mary, who turned hard work into land, legacy, and longevity. The steady strength of Mom, who led with poise, purpose, and professionalism. The unapologetic strength of Granny, who saw greatness in me before I could even name it. Though she didn't live to see all that I would become, she saw enough to know I would keep rising. And I have.

Courage to Stand Tall

You cannot fulfill your calling in rooms that punish your confidence. You cannot soar in spaces that resent your wings. Strength does not need to be softened. Resilience does not require an apology. You were made to rise. And every time you hold your head high, you honor the women who lifted it first.

Life Application

- **Surround yourself with people who see your light.** They will want you to shine brighter, not dim your glow to protect their ego. Build your circle with those who can celebrate you, challenge you, and stand beside you, not those who compete with you in silence.

- **Stop apologizing for being the one who shows up prepared.** Stop shrinking to sooth someone else's insecurity. Stop minimizing your gifts to make others feel comfortable.

- **You are not too much.** You are just enough for the purpose God placed in you. You are strong. You are seen. You are chosen. So own it. Shine with it. And never, ever apologize for it.

- **Your resilience is not your burden.** It's your birthright. Your resilience is your testimony. Your resilience is your permission slip to stand tall.

REFLECTION

Where am I shrinking myself to keep others comfortable? (Identify where you dimmed your light.)

____

____

____

____

____

Who celebrate my strength? Lean into relationships that clap for you loudly and love you honestly.

____

____

____

____

____

What gifts have I hidden out of fear of judgment or jealousy?

____

____

____

____

____

PRAYER

God,

Help me see what my life would look like if I stopped shrinking and started shining.

Amen.

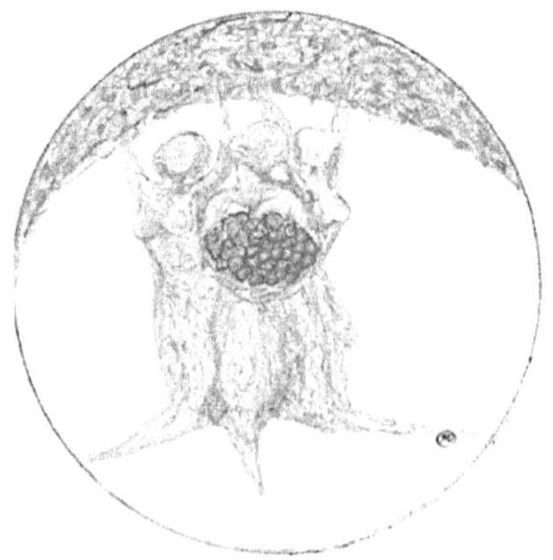

15 – NOTHING BEATS A FAIL, BUT A TRY!

There is a phrase that lived in my family long before I understood its power. My aunts shared that it was one of Grandma Mary's favorite saying, a reminder, a push, a declaration of purpose: *"Nothing beats a fail but a try!"* . It was not merely something she said. It was how she lived and how she conquered every goal she set before herself.

When she set her sights on something, she pursued it with full faith and full effort. Hard work was never the barrier. Doubt never led the way. Fear was never the decision maker. Had she shared her dream with the wrong people, the idea of a five foot four Black woman owning eighty acres of her own land would have seemed unbelievable, even impossible. Thanks be to God, she did not live her life waiting for permission. She led by taking action and understood that goals do not grow under the weight of hesitation, and faith without movement never produces legacy.

Possibility as a Principle

Granny taught me that my mind could take me farther than my circumstances ever could. She would often tell me, *"If you can think it, baby, you can do it."* She championed courage and pushed me to see doors others assumed would always remain closed. She refused to let limitation take root in my language or in my dreams.

Her belief in me became propulsion. She wanted me to pursue what I desired, not halfway and not timidly, but boldly. She taught me that trying is the only path that leads to testimony, and that faith finds its proof in action.

The Wind Beneath My Wings

My mother was the strongest and most consistent voice cheering for my success. When the world tried to discourage me, she became the voice I chose to hear. She would remind me often, *"What God has for you is for you."*

There was no hesitation in her confidence and no apology in her faith. She taught me not to shrink or second guess what God had placed inside me. She trained me to push past the noise of doubt, both internal and external, and to trust God's timing, my preparation, and the calling written on my life from birth. She reminded me that fear may knock, but faith always has the authority to answer.

The Courage to Try

From these three powerful women, I learned this truth. If you never try, you have already answered no for yourself. Failure is not the enemy. Fear is. Action turns dreams into plans and prayers into progress.

Trying is an act of courage. Trying is an act of faith. Trying is what separates those who only dream from those who become. In the end, nothing will ever beat a fail but a try, because if you never try, you will never know whether the outcome was a win or a lesson.

Life Application

- **Try**. Trying is how we honor our Mothers and God. Trying is how we become the version of ourselves they prayed for, worked for, and believed in.

- **Do not delay and do not shrink back.** Effort unlocks destiny, and you can't win a race you refuse to run.

- **Failure is feedback, not a finish.** Every attempt grows you. Silence the doubt and refuse to let other people's limits define your possibilities. Courage requires motion, and even small steps move you closer to purpose. Your dreams deserve the chance to live, and trying is how you honor the call on your life.

REFLECTION

What dream have I held hostage by fear? Identify the goal you stopped yourself from pursuing.

____

____

____

____

____

What is one step I can take this week toward it? - Small actions still count as forward movement.

____

____

____

____

____

Whose doubt have I mistaken for divine direction? - Release the voices that do not align with God's plan.

____

____

____

____

____

PRAYER

God,

Don't allow me to talk myself out of what You have already promised. Nothing beats a fail but a try.

Amen.

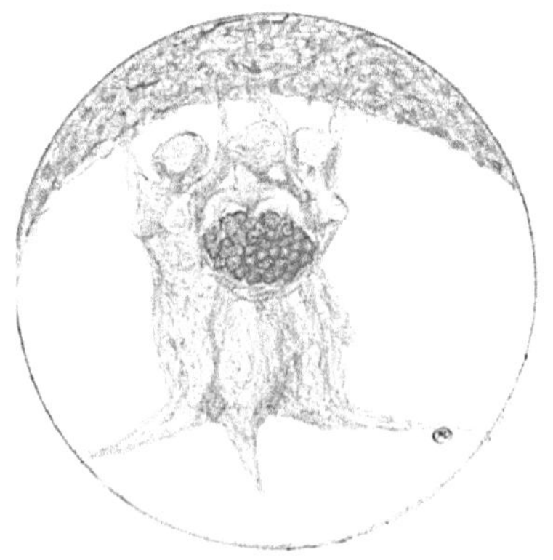

16 – THERE IS MORE THAN ONE PATH FORWARD

Success has never been a one way street. The women who raised me taught me that dreams do not require permission, only perseverance. Whenever I questioned whether I could still achieve something after the original plan fell apart, my mother would offer a gentle truth filled with undeniable power. Mom used to say, *"There is more than one path to the same goal."* Her words were a reminder that your path does not have to resemble anyone else's to still lead you to greatness.

Mom — The Queen of the Alternate Route

My mother did not follow a traditional script, yet she achieved every goal she set. She married young and was a devoted wife and mother. She worked full time during the week, took clients as a beautician on the weekends, and attended school at night. She built her future through determination and discipline. She earned her bachelor's degree and later her master's through night school, with textbooks and dictionaries spread across the kitchen table.

Some people had connections. Some had family resources. Some benefited from privilege. My mother had prayer, discipline, and drive. When life shifted through divorce, transition, and the need for a reset, she did not retreat. She did not wait to inherit a legacy, she created one. Mom purchased a home on her own and later passed that property to me. Her voice still guides me today, "Don't quit just because it didn't happen the way you thought it would."

Writing Her Own Roadmap

Granny did not drive a single day in her life, yet she always found a way to get where she needed to go. She and my grandfather purchased their home in Englewood through what was known as a Land Contract, before Black homeownership was common or supported by traditional financial institutions. When banks said "no," or when barriers quietly declared "not you," Granny moved forward toward other opportunities that revealed themselves and created a path for them to secure their home. The Land Contract was the roadmap that led them to the goal of ownership. Resourcefulness was her superpower; she taught me that the road less traveled is still a road, and sometimes, the only one available to you.

Turning Obstacles into Opportunity

Grandma Mary dared to dream in a place designed to extinguish hope. She lived in the Deep South of Mississippi during the height of Jim Crow and in the middle of the twentieth century, yet she refused to be defined by the limitations placed around her. As a Black woman with limited formal education, she purchased eighty acres of land against all odds. She did not follow a blueprint. She became one. She paid off a thirty year mortgage in less than fifteen years with nothing but faith, favor, and fierce determination. That land became freedom, living proof, and inheritance.

The Detour Is Still a Direction

Growing up, I believed success followed one formula. School, good grades, a professional degree, prestige, and then arrival. Life has since taught me a richer truth: detours develop you, pivots refine you, delay does not mean denial. Back roads often lead to meaningful destinations; places where purpose meets preparation. When the first door does not open, find another way. Try the window. Build a ladder. Knock on a different house. Your route does not determine your worth. Your resilience does. What feels like a detour is often direction guiding you exactly where you need to go.

Life Application

- **Success is not linear.** Your journey will unfold in its own way. Delays are not defeats. They are often seasons of growth and development. What matters most is movement, not perfection. Resilience can take you places privilege never could.

- **Legacy is built by those who refuse to give up when the map changes.** Your journey may take turns you never expected, but every turn carries purpose. Keep walking. Keep believing. Keep moving forward.

REFLECTION

Where have I convinced myself that "it's too late" because the original plan changed?

____

____

____

____

What dream deserves a second pursuit?

____

____

____

____

What lesson did the detour teach me that a straight path could not? Write it down — honor it.

____

____

____

____

PRAYER

God,

There's more than one way to get there, but there is only one me. Help me get to the other side.

Amen.

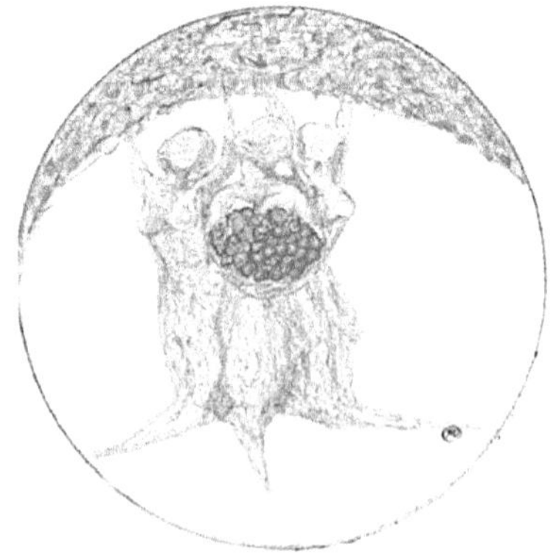

PRAYER

17 –THE ROOT OF THE PROBLEM IS THE COMMON DENOMINATOR

When the same storm keeps appearing in your life, it may be time to look inward and examine the patterns beneath the surface. This next lesson came from my mother's academic insight and professional wisdom. It was not taught in a single conversation, but over time, quietly and patiently, through lived experience. I call it

Although I am a proud graduate of Xavier University of Louisiana (XULA), a Historically Black College and University (HBCU), my collegiate journey did not begin there. I first attended a small private college in the Midwest, located in a quiet town in Iowa. I transferred to XULA after completing my sophomore year, but those years played a significant role in shaping my early adulthood.

For a young Black woman from the South Side of Chicago, life in a small Iowa town was an entirely new world. The college itself was warm, inclusive, and intellectually engaging. The surrounding community, however, was something very different. It was small, quiet, and largely devoid of diversity. I was told there was only one minority family living in the entire town, and the husband was a professor at the college. For the first time in my life, I experienced long and curious stares from people who may have never encountered a Black person up close.

Within that environment, the small group of African American students became my refuge. We studied together, laughed together, and supported one another. In the midst of perfectly manicured lawns and unfamiliar surroundings, we built a chosen family that provided comfort, belonging, and strength.

The Transfer Student

By my sophomore year, our group had become close and familiar. Some students returned, others transferred out, and a few new faces joined us. One of them was a transfer student I will call Anna. She was charming and energetic, someone who moved easily between social circles. At first, she was welcomed warmly by everyone. Within weeks, however, quiet conversations began to surface. Stories of betrayal, drama, and misunderstandings circulated, and they always seemed to trace back to her.

I've always had a soft spot for the underdog. I tend to give people the benefit of the doubt, especially when it appears that others have turned away from them. I made a conscious decision to befriend Anna.

For a time, it seemed to work. I was loyal, kind, and intentional about being different from what I perceived others to be. But as the semester continued, a pattern began to emerge. I found myself frequently calling my mother, recounting Anna's latest crisis, her newest conflict, and the next person who had allegedly wronged her. Every story followed the same rhythm, and every conversation ended the same way.

The Lesson Arrives

One day during spring break, after listening quietly through yet another saga, my mother finally spoke. She looked at me with that calm, deliberate expression that always signaled she was about to share a truth worth remembering. "Dee, you need to look at the common denominator," she said.

I paused. At first, I didn't understand what she meant. I worried she was being harsh, or worse, had joined the chorus of people judging Anna. Then she explained, "You've told me story after story about different people," she said. "Each time, someone else has mistreated her, lied about her, or betrayed her. But Dee, everybody can't be wrong. If there is always drama and the same person is always at the center of it, you need to pay attention. That person is the common denominator." It was classic Barbara J. Woods. Simple. Direct. Piercing in truth. She did not scold me. She simply held up a mirror. In that quiet conversation, a lifelong principle took root. Before you defend, discern. Before you blame, reflect. Look for the pattern. As my mother said again, calmly and clearly, "Dee, you need to look at the common denominator."

Patterns Tell the Story

That moment reshaped how I viewed people and myself. When the same kind of conflict follows a person from job to job, friendship to friendship, or relationship to relationship, the root isn't around them. It's within them. And sometimes, the hardest truth to face is when we are the common denominator.

That lesson taught me to take responsibility for my own patterns, to check my energy, and to stop assigning every storm to someone else's weather system. Growth begins the moment we acknowledge what part we play in our own chaos.

The Mirror of Accountability

To this day, whenever I find myself or someone I love caught in recurring confusion or conflict, I can still hear my mother's voice: *"Dee, look at the common denominator.*” That one sentence has saved me from friendships that would have drained me, business partnerships that weren't aligned, and mindsets that no longer served me.

It's one of her simplest lessons, but one of the most powerful. Because until you're willing to face the truth about what keeps showing up, you can't change what keeps holding you back. *“Patterns don't lie. People do.”*

Life Application

- **Patterns reveal reality.** When the same conflict appears in different places and relationships, the issue is often not the environment but the person at the center of the pattern. Patterns do not lie. Wisdom is learning to recognize them and choosing better.

- **Discernment must lead loyalty.** Kindness does not require blindness. Before defending someone, pause and observe the evidence. Self-reflection is a mark of spiritual maturity. At times, we may be the common denominator, and growth begins when we face that truth with humility.

- **Accountability is not blame.** It is power. When we take ownership of our role, we regain control over our ability to change. Choosing peace often means releasing chaos. Not every storm is meant to strengthen you. Some storms reveal who you need to walk away from so that growth can finally begin.

REFLECTION

Where do I see the same type of conflict ? Is it in relationships, work, or how I speak to myself?

____

____

____

____

____

What patterns have I ignored because I wanted to believe someone's potential instead of their reality?

____

____

____

____

____

Am I blaming others for situations I keep recreating? (Awareness is the first step toward freedom.)

____

____

____

____

____

PRAYER

Lord,

Help me see truth clearly in others and in myself. Give me the courage to break cycles that no longer serve me and the humility to grow when I have been the common denominator.

Amen.

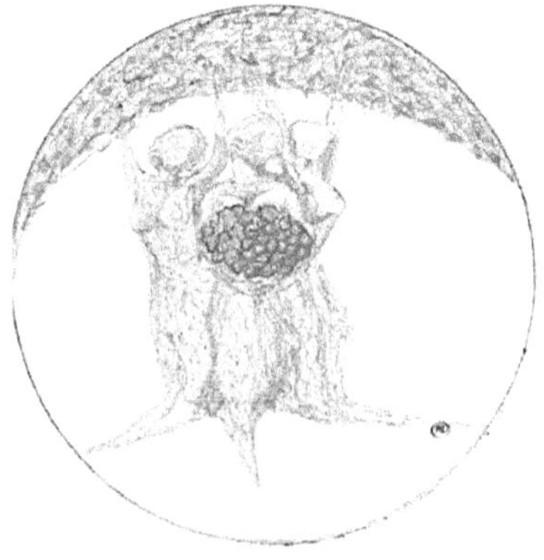

18 – CHOOSE YOUR FRIENDS WITH INTENTION

Friendship shapes the direction of your life more than most people realize. The people you allow close to you influence your thinking, your confidence, your values, and your sense of what is normal. My mother understood this well. She believed that friendships should be chosen with intention, not convenience, and built on character rather than familiarity.

She taught me that not everyone who enjoys your company deserves access to your heart. Liking someone and trusting someone are not the same. Proximity does not equal alignment. And history alone is never a sufficient reason to keep someone close.

The Lesson Begins: Early Awareness

From an early age, my mother paid close attention to who I spent my time with. Not in a controlling way, but with quiet observation. She listened to the stories I brought home. She noticed how certain friendships energized me, while others left me uneasy or diminished.

Rather than issuing rules, she asked questions. How do you feel after spending time with her? Do you feel encouraged or drained? Are you free to be yourself, or are you constantly adjusting to fit in? She taught me that true friendship does not require performance. It allows honesty, growth, and mutual respect. Friends should expand your world, not shrink it.

The Second Lesson: Character Over Convenience

As I grew older, friendships became more layered. Shared experiences, professional environments, and social circles created opportunities for connection. But my mother reminded me that access should always be earned.

She'd say, "Watch how people treat others. That is who they will eventually be with you." She believed that character reveals itself over time, not through words, but through consistency. A wise choice in friendship requires patience. You do not have to rush closeness. You are allowed to observe. She also taught me that friendships should not compete with your values. If a relationship requires you to compromise your integrity, your peace, or your purpose, it's not a safe place to stand.

The Lasting Wisdom

With time, I learned that choosing friends wisely often means choosing fewer friends. Depth matters more than quantity. Not everyone belongs in your inner circle, and that is not unkind. It is honest.

Some friendships are meant for certain seasons, and releasing them does not negate their value. It simply acknowledges growth. My mother taught me that ending a friendship with grace can be as important as beginning one with care. Choosing friends wisely is an act of self-respect. It reflects an understanding of your worth and a commitment to protecting the life you are building.

Wisdom in Threes

As I watch my daughters form friendships of their own, I find myself echoing the same lessons. I remind them to pay attention to laughter, and alignment. To history, and to behavior. Not just to loyalty in public, but to integrity in private. Friendships should make room for your becoming. The right people will celebrate your growth, not resent it. Choosing your friends wisely is not about judgment. It is about stewardship.

Your circle will either support your purpose or slowly pull you away from it. Choose with care.

Life Application

- **Take an honest look at your circle.** Pay attention to how you feel after spending time with the people closest to you. Notice who encourages your growth and who subtly resists it.

- **Choose relationships that align with who you are becoming, not who you used to be.** Determine what your wise friendships are; the people who do not require you to explain your worth or ask you to shrink your voice.

REFLECTION

Which friendships support my growth and peace, and which ones quietly drain them?

____

____

____

____

____

Where have I chosen closeness based on history or convenience rather than character?

____

____

____

____

What relationship changes reflect who I'm becoming?

____

____

____

____

PRAYER

Lord,

Shape me into a friend who brings balance, healing, and joy, and guide me in choosing relationships that reflect those same values. Teach me when to invest with care and when to let go with peace.

Amen.

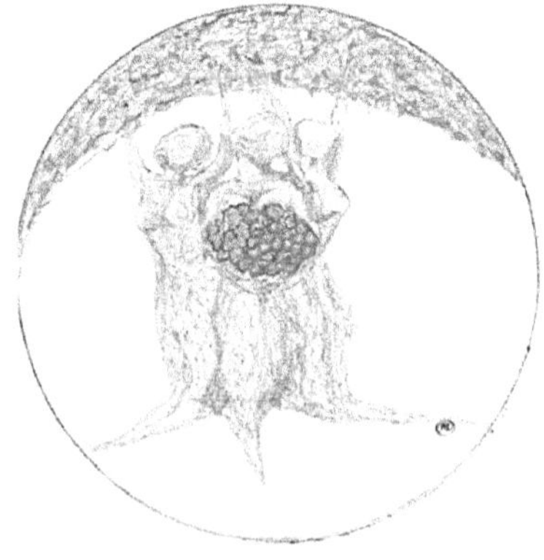

19 – TO GET A BONE, YOU HAVE TO GIVE A BONE!

My mother had a way of inserting wisdom into everyday conversation sharp enough to catch your attention and loving enough to linger in your soul. Whenever someone showed up with a juicy rumor or the latest negative talk about others, she would raise an eyebrow and deliver her famous line: *"To get a bone, you have to give a bone."*

At first, it sounded humorous. Over time, life revealed the depth of what she meant. One who freely shares what was entrusted in confidence is not a passive witness, but an active participant in its breach. They are trusted in the room because they are offering something in return, access to information that was never meant to travel beyond its original trust..

The Carrier Is Also the Contributor

My mother's translation was simple: If someone keeps bringing bones to you it's because they are also dropping bones about you. They don't get the gossip just by sitting there quietly. They maintain access because they are feeding the conversation often with your name on their tongue. They play both sides: The messenger to you; The betrayer of you. And when they repeat the story, they play the innocent role oftentimes shocked by the dirt they helped dig up. Mom called that performative innocence. "They aren't lying, they're just leaving out their part in the story."

The Strategic Side of the Lesson

My mother did not teach this lesson to create paranoia. She taught it to sharpen my discernment. She would often say, "Do not trust blindly, but do not dismiss people either." There was wisdom in balance. Those who bring information rarely bring falsehoods. They bring what they heard and what they helped create. Their information is often accurate, even when their intentions are not. This taught me that knowledge can be received without placing trust in the source.

She showed me how to pay attention without overexposing myself, how to gather information without becoming the information, and how to remain aware without becoming entangled. The one who carries news may offer a forecast, but they should never be given a front row seat to your heart.

Wisdom on Reciprocity And Boundaries

My grandmothers understood this truth instinctively. Granny once reminded me, "Watch a person's tongue. It will reveal their truth." She believed words uncover values, and that loyalty never needs gossip. Grandma Mary valued peace and privacy over chaos. She taught me that silence can be a shield and that wisdom often requires distance. Together, their lessons shaped a lasting understanding. Generosity should be reciprocal. Access should be earned. Trust should be tested. Not everyone who draws near deserves closeness.

Life Application

- **The one who delivers gossip also contributes to it.** Information is exchanged, not magically obtained. Insight may be useful, but the source shouldn't be trusted with your truth. Healthy relationships are built on reciprocity, not one-sided loyalty.

- **Guard your peace and your reputation by guarding your circle.** When it comes to protecting your destiny, be kind and be gracious, but also be wise. The person who carries gossip to you will one day carry gossip about you, and they will do so with the same smile they used the last time.

REFLECTION

Who always brings "the latest," and more importantly, why do they always have access?

____

____

____

____

____

Am I confusing access to information and gossip with friendship?

____

____

____

____

How can I model integrity in my conversations about others?

____

____

____

____

PRAYER

Lord,

    Help me hear what is true, discern what is harmful, and stay close only to those who carry peace — not bones.

                                     Amen.

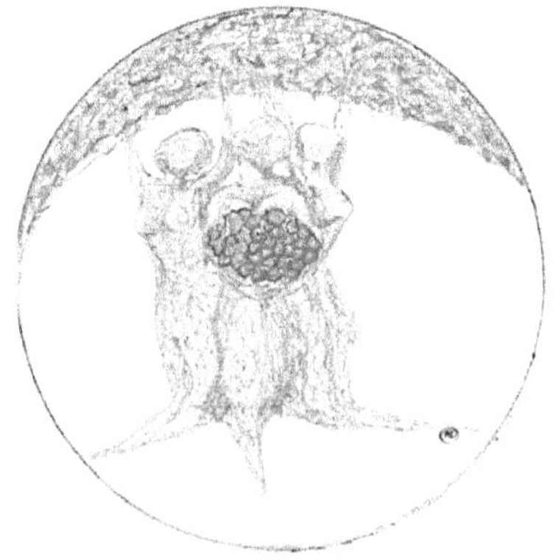

20 - ALWAYS SHOW APPRECIATION AND GRATITUDE

My mother and both of my grandmothers believed deeply in the power of good manners and genuine gratitude. Mom used to say, "Gratitude isn't just good manners, it's good living. You don't say thank you because someone needs to hear it, you say thank you because you need to feel it."

In their eyes, saying please and thank you wasn't simply about politeness, it was a reflection of character, humility, and respect. But they also taught me that words alone weren't enough. Gratitude had to be shown, not just spoken.

The Discipline of Gratitude

Because I was an only child and the only grandchild to her parents, my mother was thoughtful and intentional about the lessons she instilled in me. She was mindful of the possibility that I could grow up expecting things simply because they came easily or assuming that my desires would always be met on demand. She wanted to ensure that entitlement never took root.

Instead, my mother emphasized appreciation and gratitude at every stage of my upbringing. She was deliberate in teaching me that blessings are given, not owed, and that nothing good should ever be taken for granted. She wanted me to understand that favor is not automatic and that gratitude is a discipline, one that shapes character as much as circumstance. Whether it was a gift, a compliment, or an act of kindness, she made sure I understood that appreciation was not optional, it was expected.

Even when I earned my achievements through hard work, she reminded me that recognition is a privilege, not a guarantee. She taught me that expressing gratitude is not about meeting someone else's expectation, but about grounding yourself in humility and awareness. That lesson became a compass for how I move through the world.

Gratitude in Action

My grandmothers echoed that same truth. Although Grandma Mary owned a large farm and was able to provide for her family and others, she never took her blessings for granted. She remained humble and consistently expressed gratitude to those who employed her, recognizing that their trust and opportunities helped make her achievements possible. Her humility earned her respect and recognition throughout the community, and it is why people welcomed her into their private homes and businesses..

Granny, who always carried herself with poise and polish, was also a living example of extending grace in every interaction. During our Saturday morning shopping trips together, I watched her express appreciation for even the simplest courtesies, such as someone holding a door. She believed that acknowledgment was a ministry, and that making others feel seen was one of life's simplest yet most sacred gifts.

From her and Grandma Mary, I learned that gratitude is not seasonal. It is not reserved for holidays or grand gestures. It is a daily rhythm, a way of moving through life with grace and humility.

The Gratitude Chain

As I grew older, I came to understand that gratitude also means recognizing unseen sacrifices. It includes the teachers who challenge you, the mentors who guide you, the colleagues who support you, and the family members who quietly pray for you. Each deserves acknowledgment, not because they expect it, but because gratitude honors their investment.

Gratitude changes things. It softens hearts, repairs relationships, and opens doors that hard work alone cannot unlock. When we express gratitude sincerely, we not only honor others, we also remind ourselves that we are never self-made. Every success reflects someone's belief, someone's time, and someone's willingness to pour into us along the way.

Living Thanks

Today, I intentionally pass this lesson of gratitude on to my daughters. My Mother's teachings still echo in my spirit, "Always say please. Always say thank you. Most of all, let gratitude be evident in how you live." Because of her example, I now express gratitude with intention. I write the note. I make the call. I offer the compliment. I look for ways to give back.

Gratitude is more than courtesy. It is a form of love and a spiritual posture that keeps us humble enough to receive and generous enough to give. Just as my mother taught me, I now teach my daughters what both Grandma Mary and Granny believed deeply. Gratitude is not only about good manners. It is about good living. When you live in gratitude, you live in peace.

Life Application

- **Gratitude must be lived.** Appreciation honors people and sacrifices behind your blessings. Saying "thank you" shapes humility and strengthens character.

- **Blessings are never owed; they are gifts that deserve acknowledgment.** A grateful heart attracts favor, deepens relationships, and keeps pride in check.

- **True gratitude is rooted in awareness, not abundance.** Gratitude is not a response to having more, it's the reason we recognize that what we have is enough.

- **Gratitude is the language of legacy.** It keeps your spirit grounded in truth:

- **Begin and end each day naming gratitude.** Show appreciation through notes, texts, or intentional acts of service.

- **Acknowledge those whose work is often invisible.** Pay forward the blessings you've received.

REFLECTION

Who has quietly invested in my growth?

____

____

____

____

Have I thanked those whose love, labor, or leadership
helped me succeed?

____

____

____

____

How can gratitude reshape the way I show up in
relationships and communities?

____

____

____

____

PRAYER

God,

Today, I choose to notice the goodness around me, honor the people who bless my life, and reflect gratitude through my words and my actions.

Amen.

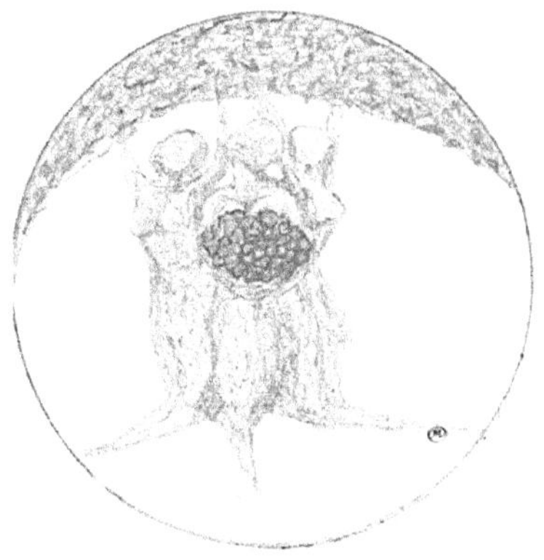

LEGACY & LONGEVITY

21 - JUST KEEP LIVING!

My mother often said, *"Just keep living!,"* sometimes with a sigh, sometimes with a smile, and sometimes with that knowing look only she could give. At first, I thought it was simply a phrase you use when you have run out of advice. Over time, however, I came to understand that those three simple words carried the weight of her entire worldview. "Just keep living!" meant that time would teach me what I did not yet know. It meant that grace would meet me where wisdom had not yet arrived. Most of all, it meant that experience would become my greatest teacher.

The Meaning Behind the Words

When you just keep living, you realize that time is the great equalizer. The things that seem certain at twenty will look different at forty and entirely new again at sixty. Life has a way of humbling you, healing you, and teaching lessons that no degree, mentor, or sermon could ever deliver. Life has chapters. And every season reveals something new. When you just keep living, you learn: Storms or challenges don't last, but they will teach you how to build shelter.

Heartbreak doesn't destroy; it reveals the strength of your own heart. Disappointment isn't the end, sometimes it's often divine direction. Patience isn't passive, it's preparation. Time is a gentle teacher, but it's thorough. It will peel back every illusion until truth stands alone.

My Mother's Quiet Wisdom

Whenever I was too certain of my opinions or too dramatic about something fleeting, my mother would simply smile and say, *"Just keep living, you'll see!"* And she was always right. Time gives you distance. Distance gives you clarity. And clarity gives you peace.

What once felt like an ending eventually reveals itself as preparation. The job that didn't work, the friendship that faded, the door that closed. Each situation in its own time, becomes a teacher in disguise. The quiet gift of experience rearranges what matters.

The Proof in Their Lives

My grandmothers embodied this lesson long before I understood it. Granny with her elegant strength, lived through seasons of lack and plenty, joy and loss, but she never complained. Her answer to uncertainty was always movement…forward, steady, faithful.

Grandma Mary, who lived more than a century, wore her wisdom in every wrinkle. Each line on her face told a story of endurance, of decades spent trusting that no matter the hardship, the sun would rise again. Their lives were living testimonies that wisdom doesn't come in a single revelation. Wisdom comes in layers, gathered slowly, graciously, over time.

Time Is the Teacher

When life brings me challenges, I hear their voices. Sometimes I hear my mother's calm tone and my grandmothers' steady faith whispering: "Just keep living!" It's a reminder to not give up, to not grow bitter but most of all do not rush what needs time to unfold. Because every sunrise brings another opportunity to learn, to grow, and to see more clearly.

Life's greatest lessons rarely arrive on your timeline, but if you stay the course, they always arrive on time. So, whatever you're facing, remember: Keep breathing. Keep believing. Keep living. Because time will show you what faith already knows—everything works together, eventually.

Life Application

- **Experience is the greatest teacher you will ever have.** What feels devastating today will become wisdom tomorrow. Time matures your faith and clarifies your priorities. Every season shapes you differently, don't rush the unfolding.

- **Keep going and never stop.** Life keeps blessing those who stay in the fight. Wisdom is earned by enduring what once confuses you. Your call to action: Keep breathing, believing, and becoming. Do not quit before the breakthrough.

- **Do not judge the story before the chapter ends.** Life always makes more sense in hindsight, and the best clarity comes when you simply keep living.

REFLECTION

What challenges am I facing now that might look different with time?

____

____

____

____

____

What wisdom has life already taught me that I didn't understand before?

____

____

____

____

Can I trust the lesson even if I don't yet like the season?

____

____

____

____

PRAYER

God,

    I honor my journey. I embrace my growth. I trust that every experience is guiding me into wisdom, strength, and purpose.

                    Amen.

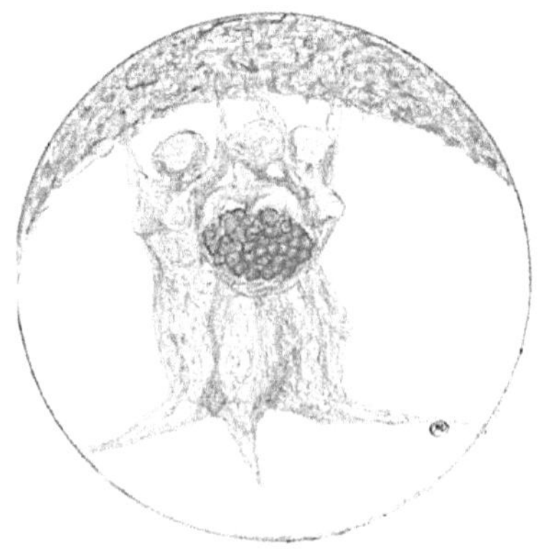

22 - YOUR LEGACY LIVES IN THE WAY YOU LIVE

Every act of grace, grit, and generosity leaves a blueprint. Live like you mean it. My mom sad, "Treat others the way you want to be remembered!" If I am honest, there are moments I replay in my mind, not because I said the wrong words, but because I handled the moment the wrong way. I can't always recall what was said, but I remember the energy. The silence. The sting. The way it lingered.

And if I can still feel it moments later, I can only imagine what the other person might still carry. We spend so much time defending what we said that we often overlook how we made someone feel. People rarely remember your exact words, but they always remember your tone, your timing, and your treatment.

That realization has humbled me many times. I reflect on moments when I could have paused instead of pressed, asked instead of assumed, extended grace instead of insisting on being right. Those moments don't make us unworthy; they make us aware. They remind us that every interaction leaves an imprint, and that imprint becomes part of our legacy.

Do Unto Others… Even When It's Hard

My mother had a way of saying the simplest truths with soul-piercing precision: *"Deadra, you know better. And when you know better, you do better."* She didn't just believe in accountability, she practiced it. Her life was a living example of the Golden Rule from Luke 6:31: Do unto others as you would have them do unto you. It sounds simple, but it's not easy. Especially when people are rude. Or dismissive. Or downright disrespectful. But living your legacy doesn't mean reacting; it means responding with patience, purpose, and restraint. Granny was the master of that balance. Firm but fair. Honest but kind. She didn't sugarcoat truth, yet she never weaponized it. People sought her counsel because her words came wrapped in love.

Grandma Mary, gentle and steady, poured kindness into everyone in her path. She didn't need a title or wealth to influence people; her presence was her ministry. Those who knew her still speak her name with reverence. Their legacies weren't built from grand gestures; they were stitched together in acts of grace.

Grace. Grit. Generosity.

Legacy isn't written in one defining moment; it's composed of countless small choices. Choosing grace when bitterness would be easier. Choosing grit when life tries to wear you down and generosity when it costs you nothing to look away.

One of the most humbling compliments I've ever received came from someone I barely remembered helping. She told me, "You probably don't remember what you said that day, but it gave me the courage to stay in law school." That moment stopped me in my tracks. I realized. that's what legacy truly is all about. You don't always know when you're making a difference. But you always have the power to choose the kind of difference you'll make.

The Legacy You Build Is the Legacy You Live

Legacy isn't only about the good we do; it's about the truth we own. Living intentionally means pausing to ask, "What did I contribute to this moment?" In conflict, remain accountable. When justified, stay self-aware. You may not be able to undo the past, but you can choose how to show up moving forward. That choice becomes part of the story others tell about you. My Mothers taught me that how I show up in the world matters not for applause or validation; every act of integrity writes a line in my life's record.

Live Like You Mean It

When the final chapter of my life is written, I don't want to be remembered only for what I achieved but for how I made people feel. I hope they'll remember… how I showed up when they were in need, how I corrected with care, how I shared what I knew, how I took responsibility when I fell short, and how I loved with action. Legacy isn't etched in stone, it is written in hugs, apologies, encouragement, and integrity.

Live fully and intentionally. Live like you mean it because in the end, the measure of a life well-lived isn't what you leave behind! Legacy is about how you leave people feeling. It isn't about the monument or what you build, legacy is about the memory and the impact you leave in this world. Most of all it's about the memory you leave in someone's heart.

Legacy isn't measured by titles, wealth, or public praise, but how you treat people. Words matter, but tone and timing often leave a deep imprint. Accountability is an act of love for others and yourself. Every interaction is a chance to reflect grace, demonstrate integrity, and build trust. You can't rewrite yesterday, but you can choose who you'll be today. The choice becomes your legacy. Your record is written moment by moment, heart-to-heart, through the impact you make on others.

Life Application

Practice these legacy-building habits:

- Pause before reacting.

- Respond with purpose.

- Acknowledge others efforts with genuine gratitude .

- Extend grace where it was once withheld.

- Take responsibility where excuses once stood.

- Offer kindness with no expectation attached. Every time you choose character over pride, choose empathy over ego, or choose love over winning, you are building a legacy that lives beyond you.

REFLECTION

What energy do I bring into rooms, conversations, and relationships?

____

____

____

____

____

Are there moments I need to revisit with an apology, patience, or clarity?

____

____

____

____

If someone told the story of my life based solely on how I treated others — what would they say?

____

____

____

____

PRAYER

God,

    May the life I live speak louder than anything I leave behind.

Amen.

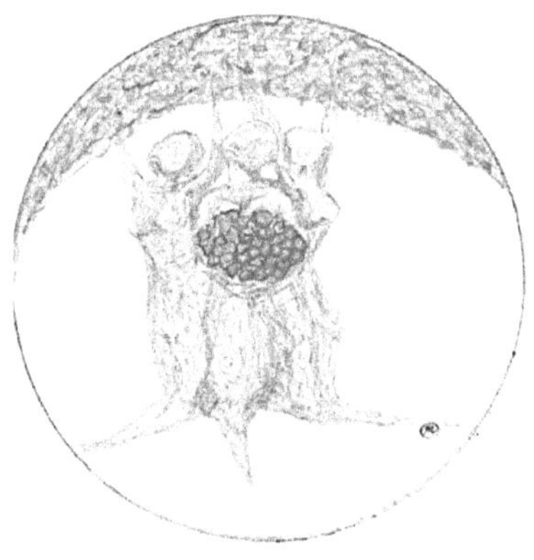

PART III: CONCLUSION

THE LEGACY CONTINUES

Legacy isn't what we leave, it's who we become. As I look back over these lessons from gratitude and discernment to faith, perseverance, and grace I see how each one connects like threads in a tapestry, woven by the hands of the women who shaped me. My mother and grandmothers didn't just tell me how to live, they showed me, through their words, their work, and their unwavering belief that life's challenges were not punishments, but invitations to grow stronger.

Each lesson was a seed planted in different seasons of my life. Some took root early. Others bloomed in their own time. But every one of them flourished when I was ready to receive it. And even now, as I move through new chapters of my own journey, I still hear their voices, softly, sometimes firmly, reminding me that I carry their wisdom wherever I go.

These lessons are not just memories; they are my inheritance. Their lessons are the spiritual wealth passed down from women who understood that legacy is not merely what you leave behind. It's what you pour into others while you're still here.

I now understand that the same strength, grace, and faith that carried my Mothers through their lives are the same forces that carry me through mine. Their lessons live in me. Their dreams breathe through my actions. And now, I pass them on to you. What these women gave me was more than love or guidance. They gave me foundation. They gave me legacy.

My mother, Barbara Jean Woods, taught me how to stand with dignity. My Granny, Juanita Love Sanders, taught me how to lead with courage. My Grandma, Mary Nealy Little, showed me how to endure with quiet faith. Together, they created the blueprint of who I am. Their voices still rise in moments of uncertainty: When I need courage, I hear Granny's boldness. When I need patience, I recall Grandma Mary's calm. When I need wisdom or comfort, I hear my mother's gentle reminder, *"Just keep living!"*

I share these lessons not because my life has been perfect, but because it has been purposeful. Every joy and every hardship have deepened my understanding of what these women knew all along. Life isn't about the easy path, life is about walking your path with faith, integrity, and love.

Their legacies live through me and through every person who carries forward the lessons of their own mothers, grandmothers, and spiritual matriarchs. So, as you close these pages, pause and reflect on your own lineage, on the voices that shaped you, and the lives that prepared the ground for your becoming. Because if there's one truth my Mothers taught me, it is this: Legacy isn't what we leave, it's who we become.

Legacy is not something you leave behind. It's something you build while you're still here. It's in the way you speak life into others. It's in the prayers you whisper when no one is listening. It's in the sacrifices you make for a future you may never see. It's in the land you purchase, the values you teach, and the love you give, even when the world gives you nothing in return.

These women taught me to lead with faith, fight with purpose, give without losing myself, and love without limits. And because of them, I walk stronger. I lead bolder. I live freer. But this isn't just my story. It's our story. This is the story of Black women rising. Of mothers, grandmothers, and aunties who sowed seeds in soil that wasn't always soft. Who dared to dream beyond their circumstances. Who built something bigger than themselves and called it family.

The Call Forward

As I enter the next season of my life, I carry their stories and become their story. So do you. This book is your reminder that your life matters. Your values matter.

Your healing matters. Your decisions matter. Your legacy matters. Whether you are raising children, mentoring a family member, friend or a loved one, chasing dreams, healing wounds, or simply holding it all together, you are part of a legacy that deserves to be honored, protected, and passed down.

So, walk stronger. Live deeper. Love wiser. Speak your truth. Celebrate your strength. And never forget whose prayers you're walking in. You were carried. You were poured into. You were dreamed of long before you arrived. And now it's your turn to dream boldly for the next generation.

The legacy continues. And so do you.

STAY CONNECTED TO THE AUTHOR

If you are interested in support for Estate Planning or other legacy building activities, Deadra Woods Stokes is available to speak for your conference, book club, or workshop. For more information, visit her website: www.timeless22-lessons.com.